Sports Law in Kenya

Sports Law in Kenya

Felix Majani

This book was originally published as a monograph in the International Encyclopaedia of Laws/Sports Law.

Founding Editor: Roger Blanpain
General Editor: Frank Hendrickx
Volume Editor: Michele Colucci

Wolters Kluwer

Published by:
Kluwer Law International B.V.
PO Box 316
2400 AH Alphen aan den Rijn
The Netherlands
E-mail: lrs-sales@wolterskluwer.com
Website: www.wolterskluwer.com/en/solutions/kluwerlawinternational

Sold and distributed by:
Wolters Kluwer Legal & Regulatory U.S.
7201 McKinney Circle
Frederick, MD 21704
United States of America
E-mail: customer.service@wolterskluwer.com

ISBN 978-94-035-0046-1

e-Book: ISBN 978-94-035-4795-4
web-PDF: ISBN 978-94-035-4805-0

The Author

Felix Majani, LLM in International Sports Law, LLB and advocate of the High Court of Kenya.

Felix Majani is the Confederation of African Football's Director of Legal Affairs and Compliance, a former sports law consultant at Portuguese law firm Coelho Ribeiro e Associados, a FIFA Pro Bono Counsel and a former ad hoc clerk at the Court of Arbitration for Sport in Lausanne, Switzerland. Felix has authored and co-authored various articles on international sports law and been invited as a speaker at various sports forums and summits.

Table of Contents

List of Abbreviations

ADAK	Anti-doping Agency of Kenya
AK	Athletics Kenya
AIBA	International Amateur Boxing Association
CECAFA	Council of East and Central African Football
CAF	Confederation of African Football
CANA	Confederation Arficaine De Natation
CAVB	Confederation of African Volleyball
CAS	Court of Arbitration of Sport
FIFA	Fédération Internationale de Football Association
FKL	Football Kenya Limited
FINA	Federation Internationale De Natation
FIVB	Federation Internationale de Volleyball
FIBA	International Basketball Federation
FKF	Football Kenya Federation
IOC	International Olympic Committee
ICC	International Cricket Council
IDDC	Independent Disciplinary and Complaints Committee
IDAC	Independent Disciplinary and Appeals Committee
KRFU	Kenya Rugby Football Union
KHU	Kenya Hockey Union
KAAA	Kenya Amateur Athletics Association
KFF	Kenya Football Federation
KABA	Kenya Amateur Boxing Association
KSF	Kenya Swimming Federation
KBF	Kenya Basketball Federation
KNSC	Kenya National Sports Council
KEFOCA	Kenya Football Coaches Association
KEFOPA	Kenya Football Players' Association
KEFORA	Kenya Football Referees Association
NOCK	National Olympic Committee of Kenya

List of Abbreviations

RADO	Regional Anti-Doping Organization
SSMB	Sports Stadia Management Board
UNESCO	United Nations Educational, Scientific and Cultural Organization
WADA	World Anti-Doping Agency
WIPO	World Intellectual Property Organization
KPL	Kenya Premier League

Acknowledgements

Special thanks go to my mentor Prof Michele Colucci for his continued guidance and counsel. Credit also goes to Prof Frank Hendrickx, Prof Roger Blanpain and Joeri Lauwers for their time and consideration throughout the process leading towards the compilation of this monograph.

Credit goes to Mr Rui Botica Santos for his precious comments and contributory ideas and for allowing me to take time off to compile and complete this piece.

I devote this monograph to my humble and beloved country Kenya and the entire sports community.

Yes we can!

Nairobi, 27 May 2013

General Introduction

1. There is no such thing as sports law. The current 'legal regime' of sports law comprises of the various rules and regulations governing the numerous types of sports, such as football, basketball, athletics, cricket, rugby, etc., that are being played in today's modern world. States do also have a number of public regulations, civil and criminal, which govern the establishment and operation and of social and recreational events, companies and conduct of individual citizens. When these companies, events or individuals happen to be undertaking sporting activities, then the public regulations so enacted by the State will almost certainly be applied to them.

2. It is these arms of the law, i.e., the rules and regulations governing sports associations, as well as the rules enacted by the State that comprise what is called sports law. These rules unlike the rules governing contractual disputes, constitutional matters, environmental issues or labour aspects, are yet to be codified into one set of uniform laws, and have not yet received the same kind of legal recognition enjoyed by these other spheres of the law.

3. However, the world of sports appears destined towards this direction. The ever-expanding recognition and reference of disputes to sports leading international tribunal body, the Court of Arbitration of Sport (CAS) has set the ball rolling for the genesis of global law of sports, if their precedents are anything to go by. This could even be made more real given the current 'hands off' approach by the governments and national courts of most countries towards involving themselves in disputes of a purely sporting nature. And Kenya is no exception.

§1. The Kenyan Context

4. Sports in Kenya are paralleled in the midst of Kenyan culture. Various indigenous traditional sports have prevailed in Kenya as rudiments of traditions and as a way of life since the history of mankind. Some of the traditional games as well as sports were widespread in Kenya. Various sports played during ancient times included wrestling, racing exercises, stick fights, hunting (using spears and arrows), board games, bull fights, and dances.

5. Most contemporary sports in Kenya are indebted to the British colonization. Proficient teams in the form of clubs were created by colonial British settlers and

Asian contractors as early as 1922, prior to the establishment of formal schools. Sports were introduced in schools in 1925. The syllabus for teaching sport through physical training in schools (extra-curricular activity) was created in 1935. Football and athletics correspondingly were the first sports to be professionally pre-arranged.

6. Today, many sports are trendy in Kenya, played both professionally and as pass time as well as for entertainment. Amid the sports played in Kenya today include athletics (track and field and other running events), cricket, motor sports, football, volleyball, basketball, swimming, handball, netball, rounders, shooting, bicycling, martial arts (boxing, karate, kickboxing, judo, and taekwondo), lawn tennis, table tennis, squash, badminton, golf, canoeing, chess, goal ball, horse riding/equestrianism, polo, weightlifting, archery and so much more. Internationally, Kenya is mainly known for its dominance in middle and long-distance races.

7. Sports in Kenya has for a long time brought joy into the lives of the country and its inhabitants, most of whose talents have either been neglected or gone to waste mainly due to the poor administration of federations, the lack of sophisticated and transparent regulations from the federations, lack of support from the government amid lots of other problems. It is needless to say that Kenyans have for a long time reaped the economic and health benefits attributable to sports, and in particular to athletics, cross country and long-distance running; the trademark of Kenyan sports.

8. The government, however, appears to have taken a side step in recent years. It has zealously engaged itself in outrooting corruption in football, by far the most popular sport in the country, and has for the first time, included sports in its national parliamentary budget. The Ministry of Youth and Sports has also been set up,[1] with its primary duty being the promotion of youth development, recreation and participation in the society. The Ministry has gone ahead to take a deeper interest in sports through the establishment of a number of sports corporations to run sporting government projects. One such corporation is the Sports Stadia Management Board (SSMB), which we shall look into later on.

§2. The Development of Sports Law in Kenya

9. There is no single law that governs sports in Kenya. Sports rules encompass a multitude of areas of law brought together in specific ways according to the sport to be participated in. The commonly applicable laws in sports are in areas such as the Law Contracts, the Law of Torts and Antitrust Law, the Law of Agency, Constitutional Law, Labour Law, Criminal Law, Tax Law issues, Betting Licenses and

1. This ministry was set up pursuant to the constitutional powers granted to the government under Art. 16 of the Constitution of Kenya.

Control regulations, the Sports Act, etc. The applications of sports laws are dependent on the status of the athlete, club or federation and whether the athlete or club in question is participating as an amateur, professional, and in international sports.

10. Kenya is a crawling baby in as far as its sports law is concerned. Despite having attained independence in 1963, its laws are still suckling.

11. Sports has, however, been practised long since the pre-colonial era. Sports such as rugby, hockey and football were played by the colonialists, albeit without the so-called regulations that now govern these sports. There were, however, several laws applied by the British in the Kenyan territory which by implication would have applied to the sporting activities that were then run by them.

12. These laws included the Bankruptcy Act of 1938, which dealt with the solvency of companies and institutions, the Public Order Act of 1950 which dealt with the conservation of order among citizens while in the public sphere, for example, by prohibiting the possession of offences in public, or and also had the power to prohibit sporting and entertainment events.

13. The first post-colonial law which was enacted, and which by implication provided for the regulation of sports was the Constitution of Kenya.[2] Enacted in 1963 following the country's independence, the Constitution provided and still provides for a number of rights fundamental to the operation of sports in the country. Among the key constitutional rights and provisions relevant to Kenyan sports are the freedoms of assembly and association, the freedom of speech, freedom of media and the right to work. These rights generally take the nature of public regulations, and we shall discuss them in-depth later on.

14. Following the Constitution were all other general laws, the English common law doctrines, the English principles of equity and statutes of general application which were applied prior to 12 August 1897.[3] These laws automatically came into force immediately following the country's independence, but have since then been repealed or amended on several occasions.

15. A couple of the English common law doctrines and statutes of general application which were adopted by Kenya have in the country's history, contributed towards the development of the country's laws of sports.

16. The Penal Code Chapter 64 of the Laws of Kenya, for instance, has been modelled around the British criminal law and criminalizes a number of acts committed or omitted by ordinary men and women who may be acting as sportsmen or organizations in their engagement of sports.

2. This is the supreme law of the country. Its provisions prevail over any other law that is inconsistent with it.
3. The sources of Kenyan law are highlighted in s. 3 of the Judicature Act Ch. 8 Laws of Kenya.

17. Similarly, the Companies Act Chapter 486, which underwent its first amendment in 1986 since the country's independence, was enacted to provide rules and regulations governing the establishment of associations, societies and limited liability companies as legal entities. It mandates all entities, private or limited, to enact to be registered under the Companies Act and to submit its rules and regulations (memorandum and articles of association) to the companies registry for recognition, and the issuance of licences to operate.

18. The Law of Contract Act, Chapter 23 of the Laws of Kenya, also enacted in 1961, was meant to impose contractual stability in as far as contracts between two or more parties were concerned, be they clubs, sportsmen or ordinary citizens, in addition to providing the penalties for breach thereof. It supplemented the then Bankruptcy Act Chapter 53 of 1930, whose liquidation procedures applied, and still apply to companies, associations, clubs as well as individual sportsmen.

19. Following these post-colonial laws were numerous other Acts of Parliament which were passed into law by the Kenyan government to supplement on the English common laws and doctrines of equity.[4]

20. Supplementary to the Companies Act was the Societies Act Chapter 108, enacted in 1968, basically to provide rules governing the registration and formation of bodies other than limited liability companies, such as clubs and societies.

21. The Income Tax Act Chapter 470 of 1974 was introduced to govern the assessment, payment and collection by the state of tax from individual citizens as well as corporate companies.

22. In 1976, the Employment Act Chapter 226 of the Laws of Kenya was enacted to control the labour relationship between employers and employees, as well as the rules governing the employment of minors, and the regulation of companies.

23. Public order regulations such as the Occupiers Liability Act Chapter 34 contained provisions similar to the common law principles of tort, duty of care and liability, which apply mainly to organizers of sports events. The Betting Lotteries and Gaming Act Chapter 131 later, another law adopted from the English statutes, was also applied, with its application in sports mainly emanating from its provisions relating to betting and gambling.

24. The Insurance Act Chapter 487 of 1986 ensured that all institutions, including those engaged in sports, undertook policies of insurance covering injuries foreseeable to third parties with whom they had contracts of insurance with. A number

4. In addition to these laws, the Kenyan law also comprises of certain aspects of the African customary law, Islamic law, international instruments, as well as court precedents.

of clubs have in recent years entered into policies with insurance companies to reimburse them for payments incurred towards treating players or sportsmen who sustain injuries while performing for them. This protection is, however, yet to extend to the public, i.e., to fans or supporters who risk sustaining injuries in stadiums either due to riots or hooliganism.

25. The Copyright Act passed on 1 February 2003 also contributed towards stabilizing the protection of the works of sportsmen as well as the logos and trademarks of clubs and associations.

26. Recent legislations, such as the Anti-Corruption and Economic Crimes Act of 2003, have also served in streamlining transparency in the running of clubs and associations.

27. It is through these Acts that all clubs, sports institutions such as the Kenya Football Federation (KFF), the Kenya Premier League[5] (KPL), Athletics Kenya (AK) and all other national associations maintain their legal existence, at least at the national level. Several other sports institutions such as the SSMB have also been established in accordance with this Act.

§3. The Development of Private Legislation

28. The first sports association formed in Kenya was the Kenya Rugby Football Union (KRFU), formed in 1923, but which was mainly run and played by expatriates. Following this was the Kenya Hockey Union (KHU), formed in 1949, albeit without any substantive rules and regulations.

29. Kenya's history in Track and field dates to 1951 when the Kenya Amateur Athletics Association (KAAA), now AK, was formed. The KAAA was an affiliate member of the International Olympic Committee (IOC) and, in theory, applied the customs and practices of the IOC.

30. It was not until the 1960s that the genesis of the so-called private legislation began to take place. The historic formation of the KFF in 1960, the AK and the National Olympic Committee of Kenya (NOCK) brought with them numerous rules and regulations governing these respective sports.

31. Although the KFF did not have its own Constitution or rules per se, it was nevertheless bound by the then Fédèration Internationale de Football Association (FIFA) rules by virtue of being an affiliate member of FIFA, and applied the then customs and practices adopted by FIFA. The NOCK applied the IOC rules, and it is these rules which have continued to govern Kenyan sports.

---

5. This is the body which runs Kenya's top flight football league.

32. Kenya initially joined the cricket elite in 1966 when they formed a united team with Tanzania and Uganda to become International Cricket Council (ICC) members. It broke away in 1981 and became a single member of the ICC.

33. Closely following these two great bodies were the rules and regulations of several other sports such as rugby, cricket, hockey, volleyball and basketball, which were enacted in the 1980s.

34. It was not until 22 November 2007 that the Kenya Amateur Boxing Association (KABA) enacted its internal regulations when its father body, the International Amateur Boxing Association (AIBA) enacted its new statutes to govern the boxing profession. These statutes have been adopted by the KABA by virtue of being members of the AIBA.

35. The rules of all these associations contain regulations governing, among other things, the election of officials, the rules of the game and disciplinary mechanisms, all of which have been adopted and modified along those of their mother international federations. It is worth noting that these rules have, on most occasions, prevailed over any state laws, although there have been very few cases in which the rules of the federations have come into conflict with those of the state, principally because the state does not have laws governing the operation of sports per se.

Part I. Organization of Sport

Chapter 1. Public Regulation

§1. Introduction

36. The organization and running of sports in Kenya is principally the domain of the NOCK. All sports federations are affiliate members to it, and apply its rules and regulations. The NOCK, however, is a body corporate established pursuant to the Companies Act of Kenya. It is in essence required to fulfil all the provisions of this Act, which is a public regulation before engaging in the business of running Kenyan sports. Apart from the Companies Act, there are other several public regulations which manage the organization of sports in Kenya. These regulations cater for instances pertaining to both civil and criminal liabilities in sports activities.

§2. Regulation at Government Level

37. The regulation of sports at the public level is mainly orchestrated at the state level. Both the Companies Act, Chapter 486 of the Laws of Kenya and the Societies Act, of the law of Kenya provide for the establishment of societies and limited liability companies to run sports in the country.

38. Almost all the sports associations and federations in Kenya are registered as limited liability companies under the Companies Act, and are body corporate, with legal status and capacity to sue and be sued.

39. All companies and associations must be registered by the registrar of societies, and must submit their memorandum and articles of associations for approval to the registrar of societies before embarking on their operations. They must submit their annual returns (i.e., documents substantiating their liquidity status) every year to the registrar of societies as proof of their solvency and transparent operations.

40. The Societies Act, moreover, mainly regulates the public operation of clubs, whether youth or professional. A society has been defined to include a club, institution, organization or association of persons, and any separate branch or section of that club, institution, organization or association.[6] Any club wishing to operate and/or receive legal recognition in Kenya must register itself as a society. Form A Schedule A of the Societies Rules requires all societies to include in their constitutions, information regarding the form and objects for which they have been established.

41. Part 3 Article 152 of the Constitution attempts to regulate sports organizations by providing for the appointment of not fewer than fourteen and not more than twenty-two Cabinet Secretaries who are accountable individually, and collectively, to the President for the exercise of their powers and the performance of their functions. It is presumed that some of the functions to be undertaken by the Cabinet Secretaries include overseeing the running and operations of the Ministry of Youth and Sports, whose activities as we shall see later, are rather administrative rather than jurisdictional or authoritative over the federations.

42. In addition, the Constitution under Articles 36 and 37 recognizes the freedom of assembly and association, which are, needless to say, one of the most fundamental elements and rights required of any sports institution. The rights derived from this section have paved the way for the assembly of clubs, federations and associations.

§3. Public Liability in Kenyan Sports

I. Civil Liability

43. Are Kenyan sportsmen and institutions subject to tortuous liability for any acts or omissions done in the course of their professions? History has at least established very few cases where these subjects have been sued for tortuous liability.

44. Until recently, torts were never a part of the landscape of sports law. However, in 1975 an Illinois' appeals court established the notion that players can be found guilty of negligence if their actions are deliberate, wilful or with a reckless disregard for the safety of another player so as to cause injury to that player. Negligence torts are typically harder to prove in contact sports, where violent actions and injuries are more common and thus more expected (assumption of risk or self-defence).

45. Spectators can also sue for negligence if their injuries could not have been expected (not foreseeable) given the nature of the sporting event they were attending. A cricket fan sitting in the bleachers would reasonably expect a cricket ball to come towards the seat, but a wrestling fan sitting courtside would not reasonably expect a wrestler to come flying his or her way.

46. Sports' tort law extends into other less obvious areas. Team doctors could be liable for medical malpractice, a form of negligence, for giving a player a false clean

6. Section 4(c), Betting Lotteries and Gaming Act, Ch. 131 laws of Kenya.

bill of health just so that player may continue to perform. A player who purposefully causes bodily harm to another athlete, coach or spectator may be guilty of committing an intentional tort along with a criminal act of assault and battery. The law of defamation protects a person's good character or reputation. The publication of false information about a well-known athlete (public figure) may be actionable if it was published with a reckless disregard for the truth or actual malice. The growth of non-traditional media outlets, for example, web pages, instant messaging, cable, etc. has added a new dynamic to this area of the law.

47. Closely related to the subject of torts in some ways is the area of publicity rights. While the tort of defamation protects a person's reputation, the right of publicity permits a person to commercially exploit his or her likeness, name and image. This area of sports law includes trademarks, trade names, domain names and even copyrights.

48. It thus remains that clubs and sportsmen are subject to liability for any torts committed by them in the course of their work, like any other legal entity or a natural person under the Kenyan (common law) law of tort.

II. Public Regulation of Criminal Liability

49. The Kenyan public regulations also provide for criminal liability, which could attach to organizers and sportsmen practising in Kenya. These liabilities come in different forms, based on the nature, wording and idea behind the public regulation or regulations that has been enacted to cater for certain conduct or omissions.

III. Assault

50. Players engaging in violently reckless tackles or fights leading to actual or grievous bodily harm face the possibility of criminal charges in the Kenyan law courts.

51. Section 250 of the Kenyan Penal Code strictly provides that any person who assaults another is guilty of a misdemeanour and is liable to imprisonment for five years, with or without corporal punishment. In addition, under section 252, assaulting, striking or wounding any person lawfully authorized in or on account of the execution of his duty is a misdemeanour punishable with a seven-year jail term.

IV. Corruption, Abuse of Office and Match-Fixing

52. Public regulation, via section 101 of the Penal Code, prohibits the doing or direction by employees within the public service of actions to be done in abuse of the authority of his or her office, or the direction of any arbitrary act prejudicial to the rights other people. Such actions amount to misdemeanours.

53. Under subsection 2 of the Penal Code, if the act in question is done or directed to be done for the purpose of gain, the person so directing is guilty of a felony and is liable to imprisonment for three years. This is a law that could very well be applied to cases of match-fixing and corruption among sports officials.

54. Furthermore, organizers, club officials and members of federations who misappropriate, embezzle or miss allocate funds meant for the promotion of sporting events in their capacity as officials, could be termed as having abused their office, and may end up on the wrong side of public regulation, i.e., The Anti-Corruption and Economic Crimes Act Chapter 3 of 2003 Laws of Kenya.

55. In a similar fashion, under section 14.1 of the Betting, Lotteries and Gaming Act, Chapter 131 Laws of Kenya, the advancing, furnishing or receiving of money for the purpose of establishing or conducting the business of unlicensed betting premises is an offence and can be compared in similar terms to the reception of bribes by referees (as people in positions of trust), players, coaches or match officials to fix the outcome of sporting events. This could attract fines of up to Kenyan shilling (Ksh) 10,000, depending on the severity of the offence, or imprisonment for a term not exceeding one year or both.

56. All the aforesaid acts could, in a nutshell, be termed as corruption, which has its place in section 2 of the Anti-Corruption and Economic Crimes Act Chapter 3 of 2003 Laws of Kenya, having been defined to include bribery, fraud, embezzlement or misappropriation of public funds, abuse of office, breach of trust and dishonesty in connection with tax or the election of public officials.

V. Manslaughter

57. Certain sportsmen, such as boxers could also find themselves on the wrong end of the public laws, should they cause the death of their colleagues in the course of engaging in a boxing contest, regardless of whether or not they had intentions of so doing.

58. Under section 202 of the Penal Code, any person who, by an unlawful act or omission, causes the death of another person is guilty of the felony termed manslaughter. Under section 202.2 of the Penal Code, manslaughter is defined as an unlawful omission amounting to culpable negligence to discharge a duty tending to the preservation of life or health, whether such an omission is or is not accompanied by an intention to cause death or bodily harm.

VI. Hooliganism and Crowd Trouble

59. As with most other countries, Kenya is no exception to the ills and evils infesting the world of sports in the form of hooliganism. There is no specific law curbing hooliganism per se, but these laws could by implication be applied to sports through certain public order offences that have been criminalized by Kenyan legislation.

60. The Kenyan police commissioner is empowered by law to prohibit the holding or continuance thereof in any area, of any race meeting, sporting event or entertainment of any other description if it appears to him that serious public disorder is likely to arise at or on the occasion of such events, by issuing a notice addressed to the promoter, organizer or manager of such events.

61. Failure by the organizer of such a sporting event to heed such a notice gives rise to an offence. In addition, under section 7 of the Public Order Act, any police officer is empowered to disperse any gathering that threatens to hold the prohibited event.

62. Likewise, the public regulation prohibits the assembly by people, with intent to commit an offence, or the behaviour by people, in such manners as are likely to inject reasonable fear into the people living in the neighbourhood or to commit a breach of the peace. Such gatherings are termed as either riots or unlawful assemblies and are criminalized. It is also immaterial whether the original assembly was lawful, provided that the assemblants thereafter conduct themselves in the manner aforesaid.[7]

§4. Public Organization of Sports Events

I. Sports Organizers

63. Clubs, federations and associations which organize sports are obliged to perform a number of duties, failure to which they could be liable for tort. The general common law rule of tort as applied to all natural and legal persons in Kenya includes the duty to provide safe equipment and premises, to provide public protection inside sports grounds and premises to all the participants and spectators alike for the prevention of injuries.

64. Any act or omission on the part of an organizer leading to injury to either the participants or the spectators is considered a breach of the duty of care and could give rise to a suit for negligence. Whether or not the organizer has breached his duty of care is a question of fact, answered by a determination as to whether there can be a reasonable inference that the defendant's breach was the proximate cause of the injury.

65. Apart from the English common law of tort that is applied in Kenya, there are several other legislations governing the public conduct of all those who occupy or run premises, failure to which could give rise to liability.

---

7. Section 78 of the Penal Code.

66. The Occupiers Liability Act enacts regulations governing the duty which all occupiers or controllers of premises, be they organizers or otherwise, owe to visitors with respect to possible dangers in connection with the state of the premises, or to things done or omitted to be done on them.

67. This Act equates the duties owed by an occupier of premises as being similar to the common duty of care owed by a person to all his visitors, except in so far as the occupier is free to and has extended, restricted, modified or excluded his duty to any visitor or visitors by agreement or otherwise. This duty exists even if the visitor had been warned by the occupier or organizer of the presence of the danger. The warning so issued does not absolve the occupier from liability unless, in all the circumstances, it was enough to enable the visitor to be reasonably safe.

68. There are, however, exceptions accorded to the organizer or occupier's liability for any damage or injury incurred by visitors to his premises. One such exception occurs when the risk present in the organizer's premises has been willingly accepted by the visitor.

69. The second exception relates to injuries sustained by visitors to the organizer's premises as a result of negligent or faulty execution of any work of construction, maintenance or repair by an independent contractor who has been duly employed by the occupier. In such instances, the organizer or occupier will not be answerable for the danger if, in all the circumstances, he had acted reasonably when entrusting the work to the independent contractor and had taken such steps (if any) as he reasonably ought in order to satisfy himself that the contractor was competent and that the work had been properly done.

II. Stadium Ownership

70. In general, all sports stadiums in Kenya are owned by the government. The duty to run these stadiums has been delegated by the government to its ministry of gender and children affairs.

71. However, owing to the ever-increasing demand for standard sports facilities for recreation and competitions, the ministry decided to establish the SSMB to whom it delegated the responsibility to effectively and manage sports facilities, among other duties as we shall see hereunder.

III. The Sports Stadia Management Board (SSMB)

72. This is a state corporation deriving its legal status vide Kenya Legal Notice No. 180 of 15 November 2002. It was established in 2002 and draws its mandate from the SSMB Order 2002. Its vision and mission is to be the preferred providers of sports and recreational facilities and services in Kenya as well as to develop markets and manage sporting and recreational facilities to the satisfaction of stakeholders and by offering consultancy and advisory services in the sports and recreation business.

73. Its core duties as mandated by the government through the ministry of youth and gender are to:

(a) provide effective and efficient management of sports facilities;
(b) foresee the proper marketing and maximum utilization of sports facilities by Kenyans;
(c) plan and expand all existing sports facilities and develop new ones;
(d) fix the rates and charges for the use of sports facilities in Kenya;
(e) collect fees accruing from sports facilities;
(f) collaborate with local public, corporate sector and individuals for timely and efficient service delivery;
(g) introduce innovative ways of raising revenue through the use of existing and newly developed facilities to ensure the self-generation of funds; and
(h) up to date staff training to ensure efficient and effective service delivery.

§5. The Kenyan Sports Act

74. In January 2013, the Kenyan government gazetted the Sports Act. This Act is aimed at encouraging and promoting sports and recreation, to provide for the establishment of sports institutions, administration and management of sports in the country, and for connected purposes.

75. The Act was first drafted in 2002 and seeks to address major problems facing the local sports industry, especially in terms of finances, talent development, management, coaching and the welfare of the player. It also seeks to set up a Trust Fund for the development of sport through a national sports lottery.

The Act further revolutionizes Kenyan sports by providing for the establishment of a Department of Sports and Recreation and a Sports Lottery Board.

I. The Establishment of Sports Kenya

76. Pursuant to Article 4 of the Sports Act, there shall be established a body called Sports Kenya tasked with the duty to:

(a) promote, coordinate and implement grassroots, national and international sports programmes for Kenyans, in liaison with the relevant sports organizations and facilitate the active participation of Kenyans in regional, continental and international sports, including in sports administration;

(b) manage and maintain the sports facilities specified in the First Schedule and any other facilities which the Cabinet Secretary may, by notice in the Gazette, declare to be sports facilities for the purposes of this Act;
(c) establish, manage, develop and maintain the sports facilities, including convention centres, indoor sporting and recreational facilities for the purposes of this Act;
(d) adopt, develop, plan, set stadia standards and licence and regularly inspect stadia for sporting and recreational use;
(e) establish and maintain a sports museum;
(f) participate in the promotion of sports tourism;
(g) provide the necessary amenities or facilities for persons using the services or facilities provided by Sports Kenya;
(h) operate sports facilities on public grounds in such manner as it deems necessary;
(i) collaborate with county governments, learning institutions and other stakeholders concerned with sports and recreation, in the search, identification and development of sporting talent, provision of sports equipment, facilities and technical training;
(j) identify and recommend talents in sports to national sports organizations;
(k) inculcate the sense of patriotism and national pride through sports and recreation, create awareness on matters of national interest through sporting events, create awareness on the benefits of regular participation in sports for healthy living and provide advisory and counselling services to athletes;
(l) determine the national colours to be used in national and international competitions, in consultation with the relevant national sports organizations;
(m) facilitate the preparation and participation of Kenyan teams in various international events and the hosting of similar events in the country and recommend members of steering committees for international sports competitions, in consultation with the relevant national sports organizations;
(n) recommend to the relevant authorities issuance of work permits and visas to foreign athletes and technical sports personnel, in consultation with the relevant national sports organizations;
(o) approve, at the request of the respective national sports organization, the clearance of foreign sports technical personnel before engagement by national sports organizations and other sporting bodies;
(p) organize and coordinate training, conduct research, maintain a resource centre and provide and engage consultancy services for sports development programmes, in consultation with the respective national sports organizations;
(q) with the approval of the Cabinet Secretary, prescribe charges or fees in respect of;
(r) access to, or use of, any of the resources or facilities of Sports Kenya;
(s) the provision of programmes, services, information or advice by Sports Kenya; and
(t) the admission of persons to events and activities organized by Sports Kenya;
(u) recommend, in liaison with the relevant sports organizations, tax exemption for sportspersons; and

(v) perform such other functions related to the implementation of this Act as may be directed by the Cabinet Secretary.

77. The Sports Act imposes a retirement age of 75 years for officials holding office in national federations.

78. With a view to avoiding any possible conflict of interest, the Sports Act also stipulates that an official cannot hold office or different posts in more than one federation at the same time.

79. The Act, however, envisages a possible conflict with the regulations of a vast majority of international federations which strictly prohibit government interference in national sports by allowing the Cabinet Secretary of the Ministry of Youth and Sports to remove officials serving in association and to form caretaker committees in case of mismanagement.

Chapter 2. Private Regulation

§1. The National Olympic Committee of Kenya (NOCK)

I. Introduction

80. The main body which governs Kenyan sports at the private level is the NOCK. All the members of the national bodies affiliated to the NOCK are obliged to follow the NOCK rules as well as those of the IOC, in addition to those issued by their respective federations.

81. The NOCK was formed in 1955 and recognized by the IOC, which is the main financier of the NOCK.

82. Its membership is largely comprised of the officials and members of all the national federations in Kenya. The NOCK can only recognize one national federation per sport in Kenya, and all national federations. Multi-sports groups and other sports-oriented organizations are also members of the NOCK.

83. Although the NOCK is itself required, and has been registered as a limited liability company under the Companies Act, its mandate towards the public regulation of sports in Kenya has not received any express authorization from any State legislation per se.

II. Roles, Duties and Objectives of the NOCK

84. The NOCK's main role is to coordinate, guide and monitor all sports in Kenya. It promotes the fundamental principles of Olympism in Kenya within the framework of sports. In addition to this, the NOCK strives to:

(a) Participate in the training of sports administrators by organizing educational programmes.
(b) Ensure that athletes from their respective nations attend the Olympic Games. It is only the NOCK which has the power to select and send teams and competitors for participation in the Olympic Games.
(c) Supervise the preliminary selection of potential bid cities.

85. The NOCK's authority extends to all the country's national federations affiliated to international sports federations that have been recognized by the IOC, and also to federations whose sports of which are have not been included in the programme of the Olympic Games.

§2. THE SPORTS FEDERATIONS

86. As a sporting nation, Kenya has numerous federations established at the national level to run various types of sports. Some of the federations so established include the Kenya Motor Sport Federation, the Kenya Rowing and Canoe Association, the Kenya Motor Sport Federation, the Kenya Lawn Tennis Association, the KABA, the Kenya Cricket Association and the KRFU, just to name but a few.

87. However, the most popular sports are football, volleyball, basketball and athletics. These sports are respectively run by the Football Kenya Federation (FKF), the Kenya Swimming Federation (KSF), the Kenya Volleyball Federation (KVF), the Kenya Basketball Federation (KBF) and AK.

I. Status of National Federations

88. With the exception of the FKF, which is an association limited by guarantee incorporated and registered under the Companies Act Chapter 486 Laws of Kenya and is registered for an unlimited period with its operations being governed by the laws of Kenya and the FKF Statutes, sports federations in Kenya generally take the form of non-governmental and non-political organizations registered under the Societies Act cap 108 Laws of Kenya. Their Statutes prohibit any form of religious, sexual, ethnic or racial discrimination.

89. They vest themselves with power to govern the respective national sport, and represent it at the international level.

II. Appointment and Replacement of Officials

90. Officials are appointed and replaced at different intervals depending on the provisions contained in the relevant statutes of the federation which governs a particular sport.

91. Kenyan football, for example, holds its elections at an annual level. Elections may, however, be held twice or even more than twice a year, if the members of Football Kenya convene a special general meeting with elections as the specific agenda. However, this rarely happens.

92. Other sports such as basketball hold their elections every four years. Basketball officials can only hold office for a maximum period of four years, although they are not restricted from seeking re-election prior to the lapse of these four years (Article 25.4 of the KBF Statutes). There are no such limits in Kenyan football.

93. Officials in Kenyan sports are replaced by way of a secret ballot during the federations' annual general meeting.

94. Only duly valid and recognized delegates are entitled to vote. The delegates are themselves nominated from the various branches (regions) in Kenya and each have one ballot. For example, as of 2011, Kenyan football was comprised of seventeen branches.

95. The results thereof are only valid if the said annual general meeting is attended by not less than two-thirds of the members who are entitled to vote. This is specifically the case with Kenyan football.[8]

96. In order to be successfully elected as an official in a Kenyan sports federation, a candidate must garner an absolute majority of the votes cast and be recorded as valid (50% + 1). In case none of the candidates garners an absolute majority, then a second round of votes shall be cast, and the one with the highest votes is declared winner on the basis of a simple majority.

97. If there are more than two candidates for more than one available position, the candidate that obtains the lowest number of votes is eliminated as from the second ballot until only two candidates are left.

III. The Football Kenya Federation

A. Introduction

98. The FKF was established in 1960 as the KFF. The KFF over the years evolved and changed its name to the FKF in 2012 following endless disputes between rival factions seeking to assert their authority and power over Kenyan football.

B. Roles, Duties and Objectives of the FKF

99. Pursuant to Article 2 of the FKF Statutes, the duties and objectives of the FKF are:

(a) to improve the game of football constantly and promote, regulate and control it throughout the territory of FKF in the light of fair play and its unifying, educational, cultural and humanitarian values, particularly through youth and development programmes;
(b) to organize competitions in association Football in all its forms at a national level, by defining precisely, as required, the areas of authority conceded to the various leagues of which it is composed;
(c) to draw up regulations and provisions and ensure their enforcement;
(d) to protect the interests of its Members;

8. Art. 23.1 of the FKF Statutes.

(e) to respect and prevent any infringement of the statutes, regulations, directives and decisions of FIFA, the Confederation of African Football (CAF), the Council of East and Central African Football (CECAFA) and FKF as well as the Laws of the Game and to ensure that these are also respected by its Members;
(f) to prevent all methods or practices which might jeopardize the integrity of matches or competitions or give rise to abuse of association Football;
(g) to control and supervise all public friendly football matches played by its members in or outside Kenya;
(h) to manage international sporting relations connected with association Football in all its forms; and
(i) to host competitions at international and other levels.

C. Government Interference and FIFA Bans

100. Kenyan football is no stranger to government interference and sanctions from the world governing body FIFA.

101. For over six years starting from 2006, the KFF was embroiled in a legal battle with the FKF (previously known as Football Kenya Limited FKL) over who had the right and authority to run Kenyan football. With a bid to resolve this, the government, through its then minister Mr Ochilo Ayacko, formed an interim committee to run football in Kenya. This led to FIFA suspending Kenyan football and their clubs from all international competition in 2006 for citing government interference, and the two parties later reached an agreement with the Kenyan government to ensure the federation's independence.

102. In 2008, FIFA recognized the FKL and this led the KFF to file legal proceedings against FIFA and the FKL, arguing that the former had failed to recognize the KFF before the CAS.

103. On 27 April 2010, CAS dismissed the KFF's appeal and asked FIFA to continue recognizing FKL as the governing body of Kenyan football. Following an election called by FIFA, the KFF was disbanded and replaced by FKL in 2011, now the FKF.[9]

104. In 2021, Kenya's Sports Cabinet Secretary Ambassador Amina Mohamed ordered an audit into the finances of FKF after the federation was accused of embezzling over 244 million shillings (about USD 2.17) of State money given to the men's national team for the 2019 Africa Cup of Nation finals. The Sports Cabinet Secretary later disbanded FKF in November 2021 and set up a caretaker committee to run football affairs in the country in the interim. This was followed by then FKF President Nick Mwendwa being arrested and charged with corruption and fraudulently acquiring public property belonging to the federation. The court handed Mr

9. CAS 2008/O/1808 *KFF v. FIFA*.

Mwendwa strict bail terms upon his release, including depositing his passport in court and barring him from accessing the FKF offices for the duration of his case. The matter is still pending hearing and determination. The Sports Cabinet Secretary's action did not go well with FIFA, who suspended FKF from international football for government interference on 24 February 2022 while reiterating its commitment to cooperating with any ongoing investigations regarding FKF officials[10].

IV. Kenya Swimming Federation

A. *Introduction*

105. The KSF is a non-profit making organization run by volunteers and affiliated to the Confederation Arficaine De Natation (CANA) and the Federation Internationale De Natation (FINA).

106. The KSF is the umbrella body charge with the responsibility of administering and running the aquatic disciplines in Kenya.

107. It has also established provincial/county associations which operate under parent bodies with the press. The federation organizes the local competitions and enters our swimmers in an international championship. It also conducts courses for our coaches and administrators as well as officials. In the near past, we have successfully hosted two continental championships.

108. Despite the constraints that the federation goes through, just like all other federations and sports bodies, KSF has endeavoured to promote the sport by holding swimming championships for the different levels of the sports disciplines each calendar year, with the support of parents, school, clubs and sponsors.

B. *Roles, Duties and Objectives of the KSF*

109. The main objectives of KSF is to organize and control all aquatic events in the country as well as develop the sport of swimming within the country; this is the soul umbrella body of swimming in Kenya. Other objectives are as below:

(a) Raise all levels of aquatics especially swimming; tap talent by organizing swimming events in the country.
(b) Run a physical secretariat with a paid executive officer.
(c) Organize and run development programmes throughout the country.
(d) Extensive training for the talented through high level supervised training.

10. https://www.goal.com/en-cm/news/fifa-suspends-kenya-and-zimbabwe-over-government/blte21072f228b5cc8c.

(e) Exposure to frequent competition with serious swimmers nationally, regionally and internationally.
(f) Train swimming coaches at the highest level in the sport.
(g) Attainment of international status by the formation of an Olympic sport.

V. Kenya Volleyball Federation

110. The KVF was founded in 1964 and is affiliated to the Confederation of Africa Volleyball (CAVB) and the Federation of International Volleyball (FIVB).

Roles, Duties and Objectives of the KVF

111. The KVF prides itself to:

(a) conduct, encourage, promote, advance, standardize, control and administer all forms of the sport of volleyball in and throughout Kenya as a human endeavour;
(b) provide for the conduct, encouragement, promotion and administration of the sport of volleyball through and by various Member Branches or other organizations for the mutual and collective benefit of the sport of volleyball;
(c) act in good faith and loyalty to ensure the maintenance and enhancement of the Federation and volleyball, its standards, quality and reputation for the collective and mutual benefit of the sport of volleyball;
(d) at all times operate with, and promote, mutual trust and confidence between the Federation and the Members in pursuit of these objects;
(e) at all times to act on behalf of, and in the interests of, the Members and the sport of volleyball;
(f) promote the economic and sporting success, strength and stability of the Federation and each Member Branch and to act interdependently with each Member Branch in pursuit of these objects;
(g) affiliate and otherwise liaise with the FIVB, the NOCK, the Kenya National Sports Council (KNSC), CAVB, Africa Zone Five as designated by the Supreme Council of Sports (Africa) and any other such organization in the pursuit of these objects and the sport of volleyball;
(h) ensure compliance with the constitutions and other rules and regulations of the FIVB and the CAVB as amended from time to time;
(i) ensure that a high standard of the sport of volleyball is maintained;
(j) develop a sense of sportsmanship and a high degree of proficiency in competitors in the sport of volleyball;
(k) enable competitors to achieve a high level of physical and mental fitness through the teaching and practice of the sport of volleyball;
(l) apply the property and capacity of the Federation towards the fulfilment and achievement of these objects;
(m) use and protect the Intellectual Property;
(n) collect, distribute and publish information in connection with the sport of volleyball and international and national volleyball tournaments and competitions;

(o) promote and control branch, national and international competitions (e.g., tournaments, and championships as directed by the FIVB;
(p) strive for governmental, commercial and public recognition of the Federation and the sport of volleyball;
(q) promulgate, and secure uniformity in, such rules as may be necessary or appropriate for the management and control of the sport of volleyball and related activities in Kenya;
(r) further develop the Federation as an organized institution and with these purposes in view, to foster, regulate, organize and manage examinations, competitions, displays and other activities and to issue badges, medallions and certifications and award trophies as appropriate;
(s) review and/or determine any matters relating to the sport of volleyball which may arise or be referred to it by any Member Branches;
(t) recognize any penalty imposed by any Member Branches (within their jurisdiction);
(u) through or in association with the Member Branches or other entities or of itself, promote the health and safety of players, coaches, referees and officials registered with the Federation;
(v) through or in association with the Member Branches or other entities or of itself, encourage players, coaches, referees and officials registered with the Federation to realize their potential and athletic abilities by extending to them the opportunity of education, and further participation in the sport of volleyball;
(w) conduct or commission research and development for improvements in the sport of volleyball and volleyball equipment generally;
(x) pursue through itself or others such commercial arrangements, including sponsorship and marketing opportunities, as are appropriate to further the objects of the Federation and the sport of volleyball;
(y) act as final arbiter (where applicable) on all matters pertaining to the conduct of the sport of volleyball in Kenya, including disciplinary matters;
(z) formulate or adopt and implement appropriate policies, including in relation to sexual harassment, equal opportunity, equity, drugs in sport, health, safety, privacy, junior and senior programmes, infectious diseases and such other matters as arise from time to time as issues to be addressed in the sport of volleyball;
(aa) represent the interests of its Members and of the sport of volleyball generally in any appropriate forum;
(ab) have regard to the public interest in its operation;
(ac) do all that is reasonably necessary to enable these objects to be achieved and to enable the Members to receive the benefits which these objects are intended to achieve; and
(ad) encourage and promote performance-enhancing drug-free competition.

VI. The Kenya Basketball Federation

112. Formed in 1972, the KBF is a member of the International Basketball Federation Africa Zone (FIBA Africa) and the International Basketball Federation (FIBA).

Roles, duties and objectives of the KBF:

(a) To control, regulate, supervise and direct, and to foster, encourage and advance the sport of basketball and the practice of men's and women's basketball in all its forms and in all age groups countrywide.
(b) To foster friendly relations among members, officials, players and supporters of the Federation through proper organization and playing of basketball at all levels.
(c) To exercise control over basketball by taking such steps as shall be deemed necessary for preventing infringements of this Constitution and/or regulations, rules, standing orders, laws of the game as laid down and amended from time to time by the FIBA or the Federation and to prevent the introduction of other improper practices into the sport and to protect it from abuses.
(d) To prevent racial, tribal, religious, political or any other discrimination or any improper distinction among members, players and clubs: all members, players and clubs shall adhere to this clause.
(e) To formulate or adopt and implement appropriate policies, including policies in relation to the control and management of the men's and women's national basketball teams, sexual harassment, equal opportunity, equity, drugs in sport, health, safety, infectious diseases and such other matters as arise from time to time as issues to be addressed in basketball.
(f) To allot and control the conduct and administration of all official competitions at the national team and club level; to license and/or endorse the conduct and management of national basketball competitions or games where this is in the interests of furthering its mission and role.
(g) To pursue through itself or other such entity commercial arrangements, including sponsorship and marketing opportunities and commercial arrangements in relation to the Federation's Intellectual Property, as are appropriate to further its mission and role.
(h) To do all that is reasonably necessary to enable its mission and role to be achieved and to enable the members and clubs to receive the benefits which the Federation's mission and role are intended to achieve; to co-operate with, join with, or support any association, organization, society or individual where the activities or purposes are similar to those of FIBA or which advance basketball throughout or in specific parts of the world.
(i) To undertake and/or do all such things or activities as are necessary, incidental or conducive to the advancement of its mission and role.
(j) To affiliate and co-operate with FIBA or other international, continental or zonal bodies, including entering into agreements with the above in any manner recognized by FIBA in the best interests of the Members as deemed by the Council.

(k) To affiliate with the KNSC for purposes of having the KNSC recognize the Council as the body exclusively empowered to control sport in Kenya.
(l) To affiliate with the NOCK and to submit to arbitration before the NOCK and to its anti-doping agency.

Part II. Sport and Employment

Chapter 1. The Contractual Status of Sportsmen

§1. Amateur and Professional Sports

I. Amateur Sports in Kenya

113. In this category, activities are often organized and managed by individual groups that establish rules for eligibility and competition. The range of activities includes regional football, office competitions, casual weekend athletics, school competitions, etc. Whether an athlete is eligible to compete in amateur events depends on the rules of the governing association.

114. Many events formerly reserved for amateurs, such as the Olympics, were opened to professionals in the 1980s and 1990s. Of note in this category is that courts are often unwilling to interfere with actions in this category of sports as long as the respective rules are reasonably applied.

II. Professional Sports in Kenya

115. The most important aspect under this category is the relationship between the individual player and the team owner/s because the player/athlete is paid for his service. This is an employer-employee contractual relationship between the athlete and his employer being the team or club. The agreement is governed by the law of contract.

116. Today, most sports disciplines under this category now have a Standard Player's Contract, which serves as a model employment contract between the players and team owners. Many times, this contract is modified to accommodate the special needs and talents of individual players. The parties involved include team owners, promoters, agents, advertisers and the governing body of the particular sport.

III. The Law Distinguishing Between Amateur and Professional Status

117. There is no specific Kenyan law which distinguishes between amateur and professional athlete status. Reference can, however, be made to the general laws governing international sports such as the FIFA Regulations, under which an amateur sportsman is one who has no written contract earns less than what he or she usually spends in order to practise a particular sport. Whereas, a professional athlete in Kenya can be considered as one who has a written contract and spends less than what he or she is paid in order to practise a particular sport.

§2. Employment Contracts

118. As either citizens or employees within the republic of Kenya, all athletes and/or sportsmen are also bound by the Kenyan laws governing employment related issues, in addition to the private laws enacted by the federation of the sport they are practising and/or the international federation laws of that particular sport.

119. Employment matters in Kenyan sports are governed by the Employment Act 9 Chapter 11 of the Laws of Kenya.

I. Duration of Contracts

120. Under section 9.1 of the Employment Act 9, Chapter 11 of the Laws of Kenya requires a contract of service to be 'for a period or a number of working days which amount in the aggregate to the equivalent, of three months or more'.

II. The Particulars

121. Like most contracts all over the world, Kenyan law requires all employment contracts to contain a number of particulars, such as:

(a) the name, age, permanent address and sex of the employee;
(b) the name of the employer;
(c) the job description of the employment;
(d) the date of commencement of the employment;
(e) the form and duration of the contract;
(f) the place of work;
(g) the hours of work;
(h) the remuneration, scale or rate of remuneration, the method of calculating that remuneration and details of any other benefits;
(i) the length of notice which the employee is obliged to give and entitled to receive to terminate his contract of employment;

(j) any collective agreements which directly affect the terms and conditions of the employment including, where the employer is not a party, the person by whom they were made;
(k) the intervals at which remuneration is paid; and
(l) terms and conditions relating to any of the following:
  - entitlement to annual leave, including public holidays and holiday pay;
  - incapacity to work due to sickness or injury, including any provision for sick pay; and
  - pensions and pension schemes.
(m) a statement of disciplinary rules specifying the disciplinary rules applicable to the employee or referring the employee to the provisions of a document which is reasonably accessible to the employee which specifies the rules.

III. Basic Minimum Conditions of Employment

122. Pursuant to sections 26–34 of the Employment Act, sportsmen practising as such in Kenya enjoy certain mandatory rights and conditions in the performance and execution of the contractual duties. These rights are the right to:

(a) At least one rest day in every period of seven days.
(b) Not less than twenty-one working days of annual leave with full pay.
(c) Sick leave of not less than seven days with full pay and thereafter to sick leave of seven days with half pay, in each period of twelve consecutive months of service, subject to production by the employee of a certificate of incapacity to work signed by a duly qualified medical practitioner or a person acting on the practitioner's behalf in charge of a dispensary or medical aid centre.
(d) Reasonable housing accommodation, or to house allowance of such sufficient sum, as rent, in addition to the wages or salary of the employee, as will enable the employee to obtain reasonable accommodation.
(e) Sufficient and proper medicine during illness and, if possible, medical attendance during serious illness.

IV. Complaint and Jurisdiction in Cases of Dispute Between Employers and Employees

123. Pursuant to section 87 of the Employment Act, disputes between employers and employees may either be filed before the Industrial Court or the labour officer.

V. Termination of Employment Contracts

A. Notice

124. Employment contracts for the provision of service may at any time be terminated on the condition that the terminating party serves the other with a minimum notice of twenty-eight days.

125. An employer or an employee (sportsman) has the right to terminate a contract of employment without notice for any cause recognized by law. In such a situation, under section 36 of the Employment Act, the terminating party shall be entitled to pay the other party the remuneration which would have been earned by that other party, or paid by him (the terminating party) as the case may be in respect of the period of notice required to be given.

126. Section 41.2 of the Employment Act safeguards the principles of natural justice, in particular the employee's right to be heard, by prohibiting the employer from summarily dismissing the employee before hearing and considering any representations which the employee may have on the grounds of misconduct.

B. Proof of Reason for Termination

127. In any claim arising out of termination of a contract, the employer is required to prove the reason or reasons for the termination, and where the employer fails to do so, the termination shall be deemed to have been unfair. Pursuant to section 43.2 of the Employment Act, the reason or reasons for termination of a contract are the matters that the employer at the time of termination of the contract genuinely believed to exist, and which caused the employer to terminate the services of the employee.

128. A termination of employment by an employer is unfair if the employer fails to prove:

(a) that the reason for the termination is valid;
(b) that the reason for the termination is a fair reason related to the employees conduct, capacity or compatibility; or based on the operational requirements of the employer; and
(c) that the employment was terminated in accordance with fair procedure.

C. Grounds for Terminating a Contract

129. Under section 44 of the Employment Act, the unilateral and/or unjust termination of an employment contract is strictly forbidden.

130. Under Kenyan law, and in particular section 44.4 of the Employment Act, a body, such as a club or a federation which has an employment contract with an athlete or coach shall only have just grounds for terminating the same if the athlete concerned engages in a fundamental breach of a contractual obligation. Some of the acts which can amount to a fundamental breach of a contractual obligation on the part of an athlete include:

(a) an athlete absenting himself from the place appointed for the performance of his work without leave or other lawful cause;
(b) an athlete renders himself unwilling or incapable to perform his work properly during working hours by becoming or being intoxicated;
(c) an athlete wilfully neglecting to perform any work which it was his duty to perform, or if he carelessly and improperly performs any work which from its nature it was his duty, under his contract, to have performed carefully and properly;
(d) an athlete using abusive or insulting language, or behaving in a manner insulting, to his employer or to a person placed in authority over him by his employer;
(e) an athlete knowingly failing, or refusing, to obey a lawful and proper command which it was within the scope of his duty to obey, issued by his employer or a person placed in authority over him by his employer;
(f) if in the lawful exercise of any power of arrest given by or under any written law, an athlete is arrested for a cognizable offence punishable by imprisonment and is not within fourteen days either released on bail or on bond or otherwise lawfully set at liberty; or
(g) an athlete committing, or on reasonable and sufficient grounds is suspected of having committed, a criminal offence against or to the substantial detriment of his employer or his employer's property.

VI. Judicial Approach to Termination of Contract

131. As stipulated in section 45.5 of the Employment Act, in deciding whether an employer had just and equitable cause to terminate an employment contract, the Industrial Court or labour officer considers:

(a) the procedure adopted by the employer in reaching the decision to dismiss the employee, the communication of that decision to the employee and the handling of any appeal against the decision;
(b) the conduct and capability of the employee up to the date of termination;
(c) the extent to which the employer has complied with any statutory requirements connected with the termination, including the issuing of a certificate under section 51 and the procedural requirements set out in section 41;
(d) the previous practice of the employer in dealing with the type of circumstances which led to the termination; and
(e) the existence of any previous warning letters issued to the employee.

A. *The Remedies for Termination*

132. After having considered the aforementioned issues, the labour officer or industrial court may issue or recommend to the employer to pay the athlete or sportsperson any or all of the following:

(a) the wages which the employee would have earned had the employee been given the period of notice to which he was entitled under the Employment Act or his contract of service;
(b) where dismissal terminates the contract before the completion of any service upon which the employee's wages became due, the proportion of the wage due for the period of time for which the employee has worked; and any other loss consequent upon the dismissal and arising between the date of dismissal and the date of expiry of the period of notice referred to in paragraph (a) which the athlete or sportsperson would have been entitled to by virtue of the contract.; or
(c) the equivalent of a number of months wages or salary not exceeding twelve months based on the gross monthly wage or salary of the employee at the time of dismissal.

133. Where in the opinion of a labour officer or the Industrial Court, an athlete's summary dismissal or termination of employment was unfair, the labour officer or industrial court may recommend to the employer to:

(a) reinstate the athlete or sportsperson and treat him or her in all respects as if the athlete or sportsperson's employment had not been terminated; or
(b) re-engage the athlete or sportsperson in work comparable to that in which the athlete or sportsperson was employed prior to his dismissal, or other reasonably suitable work, at the same wage.

134. In all his considerations, the labour officer or Industrial Court must take into account the following issues:

(a) the wishes of the athlete or sportsperson;
(b) the circumstances in which the termination took place, including the extent, if any, to which the employee caused or contributed to the termination;
(c) the practicability of recommending reinstatement or re-engagement;
(d) the common law principle that there should be no order for specific performance in a contract for service except in very exceptional circumstances;
(e) the athlete or sportsperson's length of service with the employer;
(f) the reasonable expectation of the athlete or sports person as to the length of time for which his employment with that employer might have continued but for the termination;
(g) the opportunities available to the athlete or sportsperson for securing comparable or suitable employment with another employer;
(h) the value of any severance payable by law;

(i) the right to press claims or any unpaid wages, expenses or other claims owing to the athlete or sports person;
(j) any expenses reasonably incurred by the athlete or sportsperson as a consequence of the termination;
(k) any conduct of the athlete or sportsperson which to any extent caused or contributed to the termination;
(l) any failure by the athlete or sportsperson to reasonably mitigate the losses attributable to the unjustified termination; and
(m) any compensation, including ex gratia payment, in respect of the termination of employment paid by the employer and received by the athlete or sportsperson.

B. Compensation

135. The above remedies are without prejudice to the right to compensation. Section 35.1(5) of the Employment Act is clear that an employee whose contract of service has been terminated shall be entitled to service pay for every year worked, the terms of which shall be fixed.

VII. Special and Additional Labour Conditions for Football Coaches

136. Football coaches working in Kenya have, over a long period of time, worked under informal contracts and on most occasions spent months without pay or received partial payments. It goes without saying that they have received no compensation upon losing their jobs, either on the grounds of just or unjust cause.

137. In March 2009, the KPL historically moved to enact special provisions which catered and addressed the plight facing football coaches employed by the Kenyan premier league clubs.

138. Under the new KPL rules on coaches, a coach has been defined to include the *head coach, assistant coaches and goalkeeper coaches for all clubs in the KPL.*

139. The KPL now requires all clubs to send an officially written notice to its office informing it of any appointment, dismissal or renewal of a contractual relationship with a coach. This notice must be sent within five days of the said appointment, dismissal or renewal.

140. A minimum wage structure was set up under which all clubs were mandated to pay their head coach a monthly salary of not less than Ksh 30,000 and the assistant coach a monthly salary of not less than Ksh 20,000.

141. Moreover, all clubs must engage their coaches and assistants on written contracts which must be submitted to the KPL for perusal and approval. The terms of the contracts must be valid for a minimum period of six months.

A. Health Insurance

142. Coaches working in Kenyan football also enjoy health insurance as a mandatory contractual clause. All Kenyan premier league clubs must provide health insurance for the coach and/or a written guarantee that the club will pay the full medical costs of injuries of illness which occur while the coach is on official duty.

143. Before a coach is allowed to be in the technical area for a KPL match, the chairman and the chief executive officer of the club shall sign and send an official notification to the KPL stating the starting date and the expiry date of their contract with the coach and confirming that all the terms and conditions are included in the contract.

B. Termination and Compensation

144. Under policy 5 of the KPL Rules, a club and a coach cannot terminate their contractual relationship unless the party intending to bring the said relationship to an end serves the other with a written notice of termination at least thirty days before the effective date of the intended termination.

145. Failure by either party to serve the other with the said notice shall render it liable to pay the other thirty days salary in lieu of such notice.

146. Upon termination of the contract, the club is required to pay the coach an additional one month's salary for every twelve months of continuous service the coach had rendered the club.

147. On their part, coaches are duty-bound to abide by the FIFA laws, in particular the laws of the game and the FIFA Code of Ethics. In addition to this, they must abide by the KPL rules and regulations, its decisions as well as those passed by the Kenyan football disciplinary bodies.

148. In February 2014, the KPL introduced new guidelines aimed at streamlining the transfer market and reinforcing contractual stability. Under these guidelines, any club which desires to terminate its contract with a player must do so within twenty-one days before the close of the transfer window, failure to which it shall be compelled to continue paying the player's salary until the opening of the next transfer window. These guidelines are aimed at preventing clubs from abusing players' contracts by terminating the same late into the transfer window, leaving the players with little time or opportunity to seek new employment. The new guidelines also increased the minimum development fee (training compensation) for a player from a Kenyan premier league club to Ksh 30,000 from Ksh 15,000, and for a player from any lower league was increased to Ksh 15,000 from Ksh 5,000.

Chapter 2. Employment Disputes in Kenyan Courts

149. In general, employer-employee matters in Kenyan sports are settled outside the sphere of the ordinary courts.

150. The most popular dispute resolution mechanisms in sports involve filing cases before the sports tribunals established by each sport, or to the Industrial Court. Arbitration under the Arbitration Act cap 4 laws of Kenya is also allowed, although sportsmen rarely resort to this dispute resolution mechanism given the expenses involved.

§1. The Industrial Court

151. In June 2008, the Kenyan Parliament established the Industrial Court and entrusted it with exclusive powers to 'any matter which may arise at common law between an employer and employee in the course of employment, between an employee or employer's organisation and a trade union or between a trade union, an employer's organisation, a federation and a member thereof'.

152. In addition, the said court is empowered to grant injunctive relief, prohibition, declaratory order, damages, specific performance or reinstatement of an employee.

153. Section 13(6) of the Industrial Court Act, Chapter 479 Laws of Kenya secures its seclusion and separation from the ordinary courts by providing that '[a] judgement, award, order or decree of the Court Enforcement of shall be enforceable in accordance with the rules made court orders under this Act'.

154. This does not, however, imply that labour and/or employer-employee disputes cannot be adjudicated by the ordinary courts. The main aim for the establishment of the Industrial Court was to create a body exclusively adjudicated by judges specialized in labour matters in order to ensure the specific needs attributed to employment matters were carefully addressed.

155. Another subordinate reason was to lessen the numerous disputes which the ordinary courts have to handle in relation to other disputes. The establishment of the Industrial Court, therefore, brought an advantage to litigants involved in the labour industry in terms of speed and legal expertise.

156. Notwithstanding the establishment of the Industrial Court, it is worth noting that a vast majority of Kenyan sportsmen do not seem keen on filing their employment grievances before this court for settlement. This is attributed to several factors, the greatest being lack of sufficient funds to sustain their cases.

157. The judgments issued by the Industrial Court are, however, not final and binding. Section 17.1 of the Industrial Court Act allows a party to any proceeding before the Industrial Court to appeal to the Court of Appeal.

158. For purposes of specificity of sports, a number of the regulations of Kenya's sports bodies, such as those of the FKL, generally discourage the submission of disputes of a purely sporting nature to the ordinary courts of law. The same, however, does not apply to disputes which, even though involve sports bodies or parties, are not of a purely sporting nature.

§2. Specificity of Football Disputes in Kenya

159. Article 67 of the FKF Statutes prohibits the FKF, its members, players, officials and match and player's agents from submitting any dispute to ordinary courts unless specifically provided for in the FKF Statutes and FIFA Regulations. Any disagreement can only be submitted to the jurisdiction of FIFA, the CAF or FKF.

160. Article 13.1(f) of the FKF Statutes also requires the FKF members to 'adopt a statutory clause specifying that any dispute requiring arbitration involving itself or one of its members and relating to the Statutes, regulations, directives and decisions of FIFA, CAF, CECAFA and FKF or the League(s) shall come solely under the jurisdiction of the appropriate Arbitration Tribunal of FIFA, CAF, CECAFA and FKF and that any recourse to ordinary courts is prohibited'.

161. In general, and pursuant to Article 66.2 of the FKF Statutes, 'FIFA shall have jurisdiction on international disputes, i.e., disputes between parties belonging to different member Associations and/or Confederations,' which means that the FKF has jurisdiction on internal national disputes, i.e., disputes between parties belonging to FKF.

I. Judicial Bodies of the FKF

162. Sports in Kenya is regulated by the Sports Act, 2013. The FKF Statutes prohibit the submission of disputes affecting leagues, members of leagues, clubs, members of clubs, players, officials and other FKF officials to ordinary courts unless the FIFA Regulations, FKF statutes or binding legal provisions specifically provide for or stipulate recourse to ordinary courts. To this end, the FKF Constitution provides for quasi-judicial and disciplinary committees that adjudicate issues, including transfers and contractual disputes. These committees include (i) the Disciplinary Committee, (ii) the Appeals Committee, (iii) the FKF Arbitration Tribunal, (iv) the Independent Disciplinary and Complaints Committee (IDCC), (v) the FKF Players Status Committee, (vi) the Ethics and Fairplay Committee, and (vii) the SDT.

163. The judicial bodies of the FKF are the Arbitration Tribunal, the Disciplinary Committee and the Appeals Committee.

A. *The Disciplinary Committee*

164. The Disciplinary Committee consists of a chairman, deputy chairman and a number of members deemed necessary, with the chairman and his deputy being qualified lawyers. The Disciplinary Committee issues disciplinary sanctions against members, officials, players, clubs and matches and players' agents in accordance with the FKF Disciplinary Code.

B. *The Appeals Committee*

165. Pursuant to Article 63.5 of the FKF Statutes, the Appeals Committee is responsible for hearing appeals against decisions from the FKF Disciplinary Committee or the Independent Disciplinary and Appeals Committee (IDAC) that are not declared final by the FKF Statutes. Since Article 24.3 of the KPL Policy on the Status and Transfer of Players declares the IDAC decisions to be final and binding, it is implied that the Appeals Committee, given that its functions are governed by the FKF Disciplinary Code, only has jurisdiction to hear appeals against decisions issued by the IDAC on disciplinary matters.

C. *The Arbitration Tribunal*

166. Article 66.1 of the FKF Statues requires the FKF to create an Arbitration Tribunal, which shall deal with all internal national disputes between FKF, its members, and players, officials and matches and players' agents. However, the said tribunal is yet to be seen active and to date, it is only the KPL which has taken up the mantle of establishing active judicial bodies, notwithstanding the provisions of Article 66.4 of the FKF Statutes, which stipulate that '[a]s long as within the territory of Kenya no national sports Arbitrational Tribunal has been installed and recognised by the General Meeting of FKF, any dispute of national dimension may only be referred the arbitration tribunal established by the National Olympics Committee'.

D. *The Independent Disciplinary and Complaints Committee (IDCC)*

167. Article 24.2 of the KPL Policy on the Status and Transfer of Players provides for the establishment of a national dispute resolution chamber to adjudicate in the presence of at least three members, including the chairman or the deputy chairman and at least one club and one player representative.

168. Pending the formation of the said chamber, the KPL established the IDCC to specialize in resolving disciplinary matters. In order to allow appeals against decisions issued by the IDCC, the KPL, in consultation with the FKF, formed the IDAC and effectively granted it jurisdiction to act as a national dispute resolution chamber until the establishment of the real national dispute resolution chamber pre-viewed under Article 24.2 of the KPL Policy on the Status and Transfer of Players.[11]

E. The Independent Disciplinary and Appeals Committee

169. The IDAC is football's most active arbitral tribunal in Kenya, established and governed by the principles of Article 22 of the FIFA Regulations on the Status and Transfer of Players, which allow the establishment of independent arbitration tribunals at the national level, with the aim of guaranteeing fair proceedings and respecting the principle of equal representation of players and clubs. The FKF handles all cases to do with teams and players through the Player Status Committee (PSC), with an upper channel being the IDAC. The KPL has the IDCC and its own IDAC separate from that of the FKF. It, however, has limited jurisdiction over contract-related matters. In addition, there exists the Sports Disputes Tribunal (SDT), that handles sports-related disputes and there are the courts where some clubs and players are free to seek an audience without prejudice to sanctions from FKF in accordance with the FKF Constitution.

170. Although it appears to have been established for the sole purpose of adjudicating appeals against disciplinary sanctions, the IDAC has evolved into Kenya's football's main dispute resolution tribunal, resolving disputes in accordance with the various FKF regulations, the KPL Policy on the Status and Transfer of Players, the FIFA Regulations and Kenyan law.

171. Presumably established and governed by the principles of Article 22 of the FIFA Regulations on the Status and Transfer of Players, which allows the establishment of independent arbitration tribunals at the national level with the aim of guaranteeing fair proceedings and respecting the principle of equal representation of players and clubs, the Constitution of the IDAC members and its structure and operations however remains unclear, particularly in relation to whether the IDAC is indeed an independent arbitral tribunal established as required by FIFA.

172. FIFA Circular No. 1010 of 20 December 2005 insists on disputes at the national level being handled by an arbitration tribunal which respects:

(a) 'the principle of parity when constituting the arbitration tribunal', which means that 'every party shall have the right to appoint an arbitrator'; and
(b) 'The right to an independent and impartial tribunal.'

173. Although Article 23.2 of the KPL Policy on the Status and Transfer of Players requires the national dispute resolution chamber to 'consist of equal numbers of

11. The footnote to Art. 24.2 of the KPL Policy on the Status and Transfer of Players states that 'Until the Dispute Resolution Chamber is established, the matters in Article 22 shall be dealt with by the KPL Independent Disciplinary and Appeals Committee (IDAC).'

club and player representatives', the extent to which such equity has actually been practised is unknown, because there is no information on whether the KEFOPA, which is relatively small and in its evolution stages, is involved in the appointment of the IDAC members.

174. In addition, FIFA requires all federations which claim to have national tribunals to have these regulations to enact special regulations on the composition, jurisdiction and procedural rules of this tribunal. It is, however, unknown as to whether the FKF the National Executive Committee has enacted such regulations, although Article 66.2 of the FKF Statutes provides for such enactment.

175. It is therefore interesting to see whether the validity or even legality of final and binding decisions rendered by the IDAC can be challenged before the CAS under Article 68.2 of the FKF Statutes, which only prevents the CAS from hearing appeals against 'decisions passed by an independent and duly constituted Arbitration Tribunal of an Association or Confederation'.

176. The IDAC which has grown in leaps and bounds is widely known to resolve transfer and employment related disputes between clubs and players of a national dimension at first instance to a final and binding conclusion, and appeals against disciplinary decisions issued by the IDCC in Kenyan football. Decisions issued by IDAC from appeals against IDCC decisions are not final, and may be appealed to the FKF Appeals Committee.

177. For example, *Mathare Untied FC v. Osborne Monday and Sofapaka FC* which was resolved in 2010 involved Kenyan club. In this case, Kenyan footballer Osborne Monday unilaterally terminated his contract with Kenyan club Mathare United following the club's failure to pay his salary for three months. Monday then joined Tanzanian club Azam FC before returning to Kenya to play for rivals Sofapaka FC. But the IDAC found Monday guilty of having unilaterally and without just cause terminated his contract with Mathare United, and banned him from football activity for four months.

178. Another followed in June 2010, between *Titus Mulama v. Mathare United.* In this case, Titus Mulama terminated his contract with Mathare United and approached the IDAC requesting it to officially declare his contract with Mathare United terminated due to delayed wages, bonuses and allowances accumulating to Ksh 134,000 that were to be paid at the beginning of the season.

179. In an interesting decision, the IDAC held that Mulama's reason for seeking to terminate his contract with Mathare United due to delayed wages was not one of the grounds provided under the FIFA Regulations under which a player can terminate his contract. The IDAC held that Mulama's dues had been paid at the time of the decision, and therefore found that he had no just cause to terminate his contract.

180. The IDAC held that under Article 17 of the FIFA Regulations on the Status and Transfer of Players, a party who terminates a contract without just cause shall pay compensation and shall be liable to sporting sanctions. Since Mulama's reason for contract termination was found to be unjust, he was ordered to compensate Mathare United with Ksh 6,500 and further banned from playing football for a period of four months. Mathare United was ordered to give Mulama a release letter upon being paid Ksh 6,500.

II. The Court of Arbitration for Sport

181. Under Article 36.1 of the FKF Statutes, the FKF recognizes the CAS in Lausanne, Switzerland.

A. *The CAS Jurisdiction*

182. Article 67 of the FKF Statutes allows parties to appeal against a final and binding FIFA decision which shall be heard by the CAS in Lausanne, Switzerland. The CAS shall not, however, hear appeals on violations of the Laws of the Game, suspensions of up to four matches or up to three months, or decisions passed by an independent and duly constituted Arbitration Tribunal of an Association or Confederation.

§3. Specificity of Basketball Disputes in Kenya

183. Like football, Kenyan basketball prohibits its members from filing disputes before the ordinary courts. Article 7(f) of the KBF Constitution is instructive that all KBF members must adopt a statutory clause specifying that any dispute requiring arbitration involving itself or one of its members and relating to the Statutes, regulations, directives and decisions of FIBA and the Federation or the League(s) shall come solely under the jurisdiction of the appropriate Arbitration Tribunal of FIBA and the Federation, the KNSC, or the NOCK Sports and dispute arbitration committee and anti-doping agency and that any recourse to ordinary courts is prohibited.

184. The sole dispute resolution bodies for Kenyan basketball at the national level are the KNSC and the NOCK Sports and dispute arbitration committee. An inference from Article 36.2 of the KBF Constitution implies that if resolved, the decisions issued by the KNSC and the NOCK Sports and dispute arbitration committee are final and binding.

I. The Court of Arbitration for Sport

185. Article 36.2 of the KBF Constitution, however, grants the CAS jurisdiction to hear any dispute arising from the KBF Constitution which cannot be settled by the KNSC or by the NOCK Sports and dispute arbitration committee and anti-doping agency, or any appeal from decisions issued by the aforementioned bodies. The parties concerned must undertake to comply with the Statutes and procedural rules of the CAS and to accept and enforce its decision in good faith.

Chapter 3. Freedom of Movement of Sportspersons

186. Article 39.1 and 2 of the Kenyan Constitution accords every person the right to freedom of movement and the right to leave Kenya. Section 5.1(a) of the Employment Act specifically requires the Kenyan minister for labour, labour officers and the Industrial Court to:

(a) promote equality of opportunity in employment in order to eliminate discrimination in employment; and
(b) promote and guarantee equality of opportunity for a person who, is a migrant worker or a member of the family of the migrant worker, lawfully within Kenya.

187. Section 5.2 of the Employment Act also requires all employers to promote equal opportunity in employment and strive to eliminate discrimination in any employment policy or practice.

188. Relating the above laws with Kenyan sports, one can say that there are no Kenyan sports regulations which prohibit the free movement and transfer of players.

§1. Quotas and Foreign Players

189. There is, however, a quota system currently implemented in the Kenyan premier league football. Under this system, a Kenyan football club can register a maximum of five players who are not Kenyan citizens. An application to register a foreign player must include a copy of their Kenyan residence and work permits. Each Kenyan premier league club can only register a maximum of thirty players.

190. With effect from January 2014, the Kenyan Premier League reviewed the quota regulations governing the number of foreign players. Previously, a Kenyan football club could only register a maximum of five players who were not Kenyan citizens but only field three foreign players at any given point in a match. However, from January 2014, the Kenyan Premier League adopted the 6+5 rule under which a Kenyan premier league club can sign as many foreign players as it wishes but only field five foreign players at any given point in a match.

§2. Restrictive Trade Practices

191. Section 24.1 of the Competition Act prohibits any conduct which amounts to the abuse of a dominant position in a market in Kenya, or a substantial part of Kenya. Pursuant to section 24.2(b) of the Competition Act, abuse of a dominant position includes limiting or restricting production, market outlets or market access, investment, distribution, technical development or technological progress through predatory or other practices.

192. Notwithstanding this provision, the FKF has vested itself with the sole power and authority to sanction all football tournaments in the country, and prohibits any organization or corporate sponsor from running a football tournament in a village or neighbourhood without seeking the FKF's authorization. Furthermore, such tournaments, if authorized, can only be run during the off-season in the Kenyan premier league.

193. The FKF applies a similar restriction on any club, referee or match commissioner who takes part in any tournament which has not been sanctioned by the FKF.

194. No such restrictions exist in other sports such as rugby and basketball, which continue to act as a forum where the youth can enjoy the recreational benefits of sport and also serve as the centre stage for them to market their talents and perhaps develop their careers as sportsmen.

195. One might argue that the FKF's ban on corporate sponsors and organizations from holding any private football tournaments without the FKF's authority is an abuse by the federation of its dominant position and also a restrictive trade practice in contravention of section 24 of the Competition Act. The FKF, however, justifies its position on the grounds that brokers in the country's football have eroded the sponsors' confidence by pocketing most of the money in the name of allowances from these tournaments.

Chapter 4. Tax Rules

§1. Introduction

196. Issues related to tax are governed by the Income Tax Act Chapter 470 Laws of Kenya. All employees, entities and individuals who engage in acts or businesses which generate profit are required to declare annual tax returns to the government.

197. Given the specific nature of the sport, athletes may generate several types of income in addition to the usual fixed monthly salary. For example, footballers earn bonuses depending on their performance or that of the team and also receive some signing fees when signing new contracts. They also earn some money for playing for the Kenyan national team. Athletes usually get appearance fees for taking part in certain meetings or races and also get prize money for winning some events.

I. Who Is Taxed?

198. Pursuant to section 2(a) of the Income Tax Act, business entities, and entities which render employment services are subject to tax. It is also general knowledge that employees of such entities are also required to pay tax.

199. It, therefore, goes that clubs, federations and associations, which are the main business oriented entities in Kenyan sports, are required to pay tax. Likewise, athletes employed or who render sports services to these clubs, federations and/or associations must also pay tax.

II. What Is Taxed?

200. Section 3(2) of the Income Tax Act is specific that 'income upon which tax is chargeable is income in respect of gains or profits from':

(a) a business, for whatever period of time carried on;
(b) employment or services rendered;
(c) a right granted to another person for use or occupation of the property; and
(d) dividends or interest.

201. Furthermore, section 5(2)(a) stipulates that travelling, entertainment or other allowance received in respect of employment or services rendered are also subject to tax.

202. Under section 5.2 of the Income Tax Act, (2) 'gains or profits' includes 'wages, salary, leave pay, sick pay, payment in lieu of leave, fees, commission, bonus, gratuity, or subsistence, travelling, entertainment or other allowance received in respect of employment or services rendered and any amount so received in respect of employment or services rendered (...)'.

203. It can therefore be inferred that bonuses, allowances and also signing fees received by sportsmen in the course of their employment rank as salary and is taxable.

204. Up until January 2014, Kenyan athletes who participated in international races and meetings were generally exempted from paying tax by the Government for any prize monies received from winning and/or taking part in such races, as this was a policy adopted by the Government aimed at encouraging them to invest in Kenya and to continue their sporting role as Kenya's ambassadors. However, in February 2014, the Government, through the Kenya Revenue Authority, lifted this waiver on all athletes and sportsmen by requiring them to pay taxes on all monies received in the course of their profession.

Chapter 5. Collective Bargaining Agreements

§1. Introduction

205. Section 4.1 of the Labour Relations Act grants all employees the right to join and/or form trade unions.

206. A similar provision is enshrined under section 41.1 c of the Constitution, which grants every person 'the right to form, join or participate in the activities and programmes of a trade union' and to engage in collective bargaining.

207. Relating this to the sports sector, the only Kenyan sport which to date has a trade union is football. Kenyan professional footballers, coaches and referees have trade unions respectively formed with a view to protecting and championing their works as workers.

208. The Kenya Football Coaches Association (KEFOCA) was specifically established by football coaches, whereas the Kenya Football Players' Association (KEFOPA) was established for the footballers with the referees forming the Kenya Football Referees Association (KEFORA).

209. Section 54.1 of the Labour Relations Act requires all employers to recognize a trade union for purposes of collective bargaining if that trade union represents the simple majority of unionize employees.

210. Upon recognizing a trade union, an employer, group of employers or an employers' organization is required to conclude a collective agreement with the recognized trade union setting out terms and conditions of service for all unionizable employees covered by the recognition agreement.

211. For the purpose of conducting negotiations under a collective bargaining agreement, all employers are required to disclose to trade unions all relevant information that will allow the trade union to effectively negotiate on behalf of employees. The terms of the collective agreement are incorporated into the contract of employment of every employee covered by the collective agreement.

§2. Effect of Collective Bargaining Agreements

212. Pursuant to section 59.1 of the Labour Relations Act, a collective agreement binds for the period of the agreement:

(a) the parties to the agreement;
(b) all unionizable employees employed by the employer, group of employers or members of the employers' organization party to the agreement; or
(c) the employers who are or become members of an employers' organization party to the agreement, to the extent that the agreement relates to their employees.

213. A collective agreement continues to be binding on an employer or employees who were parties to the agreement at the time of its commencement and includes members who have resigned from that trade union or employer association.

Chapter 6. Child Labour

214. Kenyan law recognizes that children are the future of sports. It also appreciates the key role played by children in sports as far as the promotion of health, education, economy, national solidarity and social integration are concerned.

215. In this regard, various laws have been enacted to not only foster the participation of children in sports but also to protect them against any possible discrimination and/or exploitation.

216. The Children Act cap 8 of the Laws of Kenya is the leading law in as far as minors and sports are related. Enacted in 2001, the Children Act emphasizes that children shall be entitled to leisure, play and participation in cultural and artistic activities (*see* section 17).

217. Under the aforementioned Act, a 'child' has been defined to mean 'any human being under the age of eighteen years'.

§1. Introduction

218. Section 10(1) of the Children Act protects all children from economic exploitation and any work that is likely to be hazardous or to interfere with their education, or to be harmful to their health or physical, mental, spiritual, moral or social development.

219. Under subsection 5 of the above provision, labour refers to any situation where a child provides labour in exchange for payment and includes:

(a) any situation where a child provides labour as an assistant to another person and his labour is deemed to be the labour of that other person for the purposes of payment;
(b) any situation where a child's labour is used for gain by any individual or institution whether or not the child benefits directly or indirectly; and
(c) any situation where there is in existence a contract for services where the party providing the services is a child whether the person using the services does so directly or by an agent.

220. It is therefore safe to say that whereas there are laws which protect against the transfer of minors, Kenya, like many other African countries, continues to fight a losing battle against child migration in the guise of sports.

§2. Safeguards Against the Transfer of Minors

221. The main Kenyan law which protects children is the Children Act cap 8. A number of particular laws are contained therein specifically aimed at curbing child migration. These laws relate to issues of custody, adoption and child labour.

I. Child Custody

222. Under section 82(3) of the Children Act, custody of a child may only be granted to the following persons:

(a) a parent;
(b) a guardian; and
(c) any person who applies with the consent of a parent or guardian of a child and has had actual custody of the child for three months preceding the making of the application.

II. Principles Applied in Making an Order for Custody

223. Section 83(1) of the Children Act provides that in determining whether or not a custody order should be made in favour of the applicant, the court must have regard to:

(a) the conduct and wishes of the parent or guardian of the child;
(b) the ascertainable wishes of the relatives of the child;
(c) the ascertainable wishes of any foster parent, or any person who has had actual custody of the child and under whom the child has made his home in the last three years preceding the application;
(d) the ascertainable wishes of the child;
(e) whether the child has suffered any harm or is likely to suffer any harm if the order is not made;
(f) the customs of the community to which the child belongs;
(g) the religious persuasion of the child;
(h) whether a care order, or a supervision order, or a personal protection order, or an exclusion order has been made in relation to the child concerned and whether those orders remain in force;
(i) the circumstances of any sibling of the child concerned, and of any other children of the home, if any; and
(j) the best interest of the child.

III. No Written Contracts for Children Aged Between 13 and 16 Years

224. Section 56.1 of the Employment Act also protects children between 13 and 16 years old from being exploited in the guise of sports by stating that 'No person shall employ a child who has not attained the age of thirteen years whether gainfully or otherwise in any undertaking.'

225. A child between 13 years of age and 16 years of age may only be employed to perform light work which is:

(a) not likely to be harmful to the child's health or development; and
(b) not such as to prejudice the child's attendance at school, his participation in vocational orientation or training programmes approved by Minister or his capacity to benefit from the instructions received.

226. Under section 57 of the Employment Act, a person who employs a child of between 13 and 16 years of age, or causes such a child to be employed, or being the parent or guardian or other person having for the time being the charge of or control over the child, allows the child to be employed, otherwise than under a verbal contract of service commits an offence and is on conviction be liable to a fine not exceeding Ksh 100 or to imprisonment for a term not exceeding six months or to both.

§3. Kenyan Premier League Policies on Minors

227. The Kenyan premier league rules prohibit a club from signing a contract with a player who is 15 years old or younger. A contract with a player who is 17 years old or younger must be agreed upon and signed by at least one parent or legal guardian.

228. The rules also require a contract with a full-time student in secondary school to include the letter of consent from the head of the school as an annex, and be signed by the parent or guardian.

Part III. Doping and Sport

Chapter 1. General Overview

229. Doping is prohibited in all types of sports in Kenya. This is of course governed by the Olympic spirit of guaranteeing every team/athlete a fair chance of winning and protecting athletes' health.

230. The Kenyan government ratified the United Nations Educational, Scientific and Cultural Organization (UNESCO) International Convention against Doping in Sport on 25 August 2009, wherein it assented to the Convention's zero tolerance spirit against doping by undertaking to:

(a) Restrict the availability of prohibited substances or methods to athletes (except for legitimate medical purposes), including measures against trafficking.
(b) Facilitate doping controls and support national testing programmes.
(c) Withhold financial support from athletes and athlete support personnel who commit an anti-doping rule violation, or from sporting organizations that are not in compliance with the World Anti-Doping Agency (WADA) Code.
(d) Encourage producers and distributors of nutritional supplements to establish 'best practice' in the labelling, marketing and distribution of products which might contain prohibited substances.
(e) Support the provision of anti-doping education to athletes and the wider sporting community.

231. In doing this, Kenya bound itself to the WADA Code, a code which the NOCK has adopted. In order to curb doping, athletes are required to disclose their whereabouts to the anti-doping authorities. Both athletes and teams are susceptible to various sanctions under the WADA Code, such as suspensions, disqualification of results and allocation of forfeited prize money.

232. Article 74.1 of the Sports Act also requires '[e]very person involved in sports and recreation [to] observe anti-doping rules'. Pursuant to Article 74.2 of the Sports Act, the Cabinet Secretary shall make regulations for the better management of anti-doping activities and such regulations may prescribe penalties for contravention.

Chapter 2. The Anti-Doping Bill 2016 and the Anti-doping Agency of Kenya (ADAK)

233. In June 2016, the Kenyan Parliament passed the Anti-Doping Bill 2016, making it Kenya's first-ever national law on anti-doping. The Anti-Doping Bill establishes the Anti-doping Agency of Kenya (ADAK) which had already been gazetted by the Kenyan government in November 2014. The Anti-Doping Bill, among others, vests ADAK with powers to promote doping free sports, implement the WADA Code, collect samples from sportspersons and to prosecute anti-doping offences before the SDT. Kenya continues to be a member of the independent Regional Anti-Doping Organization (RADO) Africa Zone V, which is headquartered in Nairobi.

234. The passing of the Anti-Doping Bill saw Kenya become fully compliant with the WADA Code. Under the Anti-Doping Bill, athletes who refuse to give samples, documents or anything to ADAK are liable to a maximum fine of Ksh 100,000 or a maximum of one year in jail, or both. The same applies to athletes who lie to ADAK or make false statements or in any way interfere with the work of ADAK.

235. The Anti-Doping Bill also provides a minimum fine of Ksh 3 million, or to jail for a minimum of three years, or both, for anyone caught transporting, stocking or supplying prohibited substances or administering them to an athlete.

Part IV. Dispute Resolution Mechanisms

§1. Introduction

236. In addition to the ordinary courts of law, the Constitution[12] of Kenya recognizes and provides for alternative forms of dispute resolution, including reconciliation, mediation, arbitration and traditional dispute resolution mechanisms.

237. Sporting disputes in Kenya can either be submitted before the ordinary courts of law or to the relevant established sports arbitral body, depending on their nature and classification. Some of the bodies established by national federations for resolving disputes include the IDAC and the National Leagues and Competitions Committee for Kenyan football, the NOCK and KNSC for Kenyan basketball and the SDT. These judicial bodies are discussed in detail in the latter parts of this chapter.

238. For purposes of specificity of sports, a number of the regulations of Kenya's sports bodies, such as those of the FKF, generally discourage the submission of disputes of a purely sporting nature to the ordinary courts of law. The same, however, does not apply to disputes which even though involve sports bodies or parties, are not of a purely sporting nature.

I. Principles of Sports Justice in Kenya

239. The duty to ensure that justice is accessed in Kenya is vested in the State. Article 48 of the Constitution is clear, and states that '[t]he State shall ensure access to justice for all persons and, if any fee is required, it shall be reasonable and shall not impede access to justice'. However, the power to ensure that such justice is administered in all spheres, including Kenyan sports and is vested on the Kenyan people themselves. Pursuant to Article 1.1 of the Kenyan Constitution, '[a]ll sovereign power belongs to the people of Kenya and shall be exercised only in accordance with this *Constitution*'.

12. Art. 159.1(c) of the Constitution.

240. The Constitution goes on to delegate this power from the people to the judiciary and independent tribunals, as stipulated in Article 1.3 of the Constitution.[13] The word 'people' in constitutional terms refers to individuals, i.e., a person acting in their own interest as well as:

(a) a person acting on behalf of another person who cannot act in their own name;
(b) a person acting as a member of, or in the interest of, a group or class of persons;
(c) a person acting in the public interest; or
(d) an association acting in the interest of one or more of its members.

241. And, in order to ensure the supremacy of the Constitution and safeguard against any unforeseen injustices at the sports level, Article 2.4 of the Constitution provides that '[a]ny law that (…) is inconsistent with this Constitution is void to the extent of the inconsistency, and any actor omission in contravention of this Constitution is invalid'.

242. Article 159.1 of the Constitution requires the judiciary and independent tribunals to exercise their judicial authority in compliance with the Constitution. Article 159.2 of the Constitution further requires all courts and independent tribunals to apply the following principles in administering justice:

(a) that justice shall be done to all, irrespective of status;
(b) that justice shall not be delayed;
(c) that alternative forms of dispute resolution, including reconciliation, mediation, arbitration and traditional dispute resolution mechanisms shall be promoted;
(d) that justice shall be administered without undue regard to procedural technicalities; and
(e) that traditional dispute resolution mechanisms shall not be used in a way that:
   - contravenes the Bill of Rights;
   - is repugnant to justice and morality or results in outcomes that are repugnant to justice or morality; or
   - is inconsistent with this Constitution or any written law.

243. The Bill of Rights applies to all law and binds all State organs and all persons. In applying a provision of the Bill of Rights, Kenyan courts and tribunals are required to:

(a) develop the law to the extent that it does not give effect to a right or fundamental freedom; and
(b) adopt the interpretation that most favours the enforcement of a right or fundamental freedom.

---

13. Art. 1.3 of the Constitution: 'Sovereign power under this Constitution is delegated to the following State organs, which shall perform their functions in accordance with this Constitution (…) the Judiciary and independent tribunals.'

244. In interpreting the Bill of Rights, Article 20.4 of the Constitution requires the court or tribunal or other authority to promote the values that underlie an open and democratic society based on human dignity, equality, equity and freedom and the spirit, purport and objects of the Bill of Rights.

II. The Procedural Guarantees in Kenyan Sports Justice

245. Article 22.3 of the Constitution requires court proceedings to satisfy the following criteria, that:

(a) formalities relating to the proceedings, including the commencement of the proceedings, are kept to the minimum, and in particular that the court shall, if necessary, entertain proceedings on the basis of informal documentation;
(b) no fee may be charged for commencing the proceedings;
(c) the court, while observing the rules of natural justice, shall not be unreasonably restricted by procedural technicalities; and
(d) an organization or individual with particular expertise may, with the leave of the court, appear as a friend of the court.

246. In a nutshell, we can therefore say that the principles governing justice in Kenyan sports are that power belongs to the people, and that such power is vested and exercised by the courts and independent tribunals. The people have the right to seek justice not only within the ordinary courts but also through alternative forms of dispute resolution. In administering this justice, due regard shall be accorded to the need for fast resolution of disputes, the supremacy of the Constitution and the Bill of Rights.

III. The Relationship Between Ordinary Justice and Sports Justice

247. Sporting disputes in Kenya can either be submitted before the ordinary courts of law or to the relevant established sports judicial body, depending on their nature and classification. In general, the sports tribunals have jurisdiction to resolve technical, disciplinary, and to a large extent, employment disputes. The ordinary courts, however, have jurisdiction to entertain any constitutional irregularities performed by the said tribunals in resolving their disputes and, to a substantial extent, electoral disputes concerning sports associations although most sports associations such as football and basketball prohibit their members from seeking redress before the ordinary courts.[14]

---

14. Art. 22 of the KPL Policy on the Status and Transfer of Players:

> Without prejudice to the right of any player or club to seek redress before a civil court for employment related disputes, the KPL and KFF are competent for:

248. However, this restriction is generally limited, as evidenced in football, which allows its members to seek redress before the ordinary courts. The ordinary Kenyan courts enjoy a somewhat cordial and harmonious relationship with the sports tribunals of the various sports associations in Kenya.

249. Overall, it is the principle of the ordinary Kenyan courts 'not to interfere with the internal matters of registered societies'.[15] There are, however, exceptions to this principle, especially where the need to safeguard against any unconstitutional act is on the verge of being infringed. Ordinary courts have also intervened in the internal matters of sports associations in Kenya by issuing injunctions where an association attempts to amend its statutes and to conduct elections in contravention with the procedural regularities set out in the statutes of the said association.

250. The supremacy of the national courts over sports tribunals in electoral issues was emphasized in the *Salim Humra, Ismael Mohamed, Mohamed Omar v. Maina Kariuki, Hussein Swaleh and Mohamed Hatimy & KFF* [16] where it was held that the national courts have jurisdiction, in accordance with section 63c of the Civil Procedure Act Chapter 21 of the Laws of Kenya, where the association's officials 'continue to defy court orders by proceeding to organize elections'. The High Court held that it had jurisdiction to issue an injunction restraining FKL (then known as the KFF) from 'amending the FKF Constitution and from fixing election dates'.

251. Corroborating the supremacy of the ordinary courts over sports association tribunals is Article 22.1 of the Constitution, under which '[e]very person has the right to institute court proceedings claiming that a right or fundamental freedom in the Bill of Rights has been denied, violated or infringed, or is threatened'.

252. Of particular importance to the ordinary courts is the need to ensure that the sports tribunals apply the principles of natural justice in resolving disputes among its members. Any party or person whose right to be heard is violated by any independent sports tribunal in Kenya may seek redress before the Kenyan High

---

(a) Disputes between clubs and players in Kenya in relation to the maintenance of contractual stability (Art. 13–18) if there has been a transfer and/or ITC request and if there is a claim from an interested party in relation to such requests regarding sporting sanctions or regarding compensation for breach of contract;
(b) Employment related disputes between a club and a player in Kenya;
(c) Employment related disputes between a club and a coach in Kenya;
(d) Disputes related to Training Compensation (Art. 20) and the Solidarity Mechanism (Art. 21) between clubs in Kenya.

15. *See* p. 2 of the High Court of Kenya's ruling in *Joe Kadenge & others v. Maina Kariuki, Hussein Swaleh, Mohammed Hatimy & Kenya Football Federation*, Civil Suit No. 322 of 2003. http://www.kenyalaw.org/CaseSearch/case_search_one.php?pageNum_result=5274&totalRows_result=71857&casCourt=High+Court.
16. Civil Case No. 58 of 2004 http://www.kenyalaw.org/CaseSearch/case_search_one.php?pageNum_result=5274&totalRows_result=71857&casCourt=High+Court.

Court. This is a constitutional right guaranteed under Article 23.1 of the Constitution, which grants the High Court jurisdiction 'to hear and determine applications for redress of a denial, violation or infringement of, or threat to, a right or fundamental freedom in the Bill of Rights'.

IV. The Various Jurisdictional Hierarchies

253. The Kenyan judicial system operates on a synchronized procedural structure where matters are generally handled by the subordinate courts. The High Court has supervisory jurisdiction over the subordinate courts and over any person, body or authority exercising a judicial or quasi-judicial function.

254. Judgments issued by the High Court and any other court or tribunal as prescribed by an Act of Parliament may be appealed to the Court of Appeal, and as a last resort, a Court of Appeal judgment may be appealed to the Supreme Court. In all cases, an oral hearing must be held before a judgment is issued, unless of course a party waives its right to be heard by ignoring court summons. All courts, other than the Supreme Court, are bound by the decisions of the Supreme Court.

255. This also seems to be the case for disputes handled internally at the federative level.

256. This is, however, not the case with football, where, notwithstanding the various standing committees established by the FKF such as the Players' Status Committee, the Disciplinary Committee, the Appeals Committee, the Arbitration Tribunal, and the existence of the IDDC, there appear to be no decisions issued by the said committees at first instance. The IDAC has assumed the role of the first instance court, with jurisdiction to hear technical, transfer and employment related disputes, and whose decisions are final, binding and un-appealable pursuant to Article 24.3 of the KPL Policy on the Status and Transfer of Players, which states that the '[d]ecisions reached by the Dispute Resolution Chamber are final and binding on all members unless there is an international dimension which meets the criteria in the FIFA Regulations for an appeal to the FIFA Players Status Committee or Dispute Resolution Chamber'.

257. The only instance when the IDAC acts as an appellate body is when it sits to hear appeals against decisions issued by the IDDC, with the IDAC decisions being appealable to the FKF Appeals Committee.

258. Given the fact that the IDAC is mainly a body established by the KPL rather than the FKF, there is the potential risk of eminent 'power struggles' or jurisdictional conflicts between the FKF and the KPL on which body has jurisdiction to run and resolve disputes in Kenyan football, given the relatively passive or inactive roles played by the Disciplinary Committee, the Appeals Committee and the Arbitration Tribunal, and the largely active role played by the IDAC.

259. However, the KPL and the FKF continue to work harmoniously and in consultation, notwithstanding the fact that FIFA vests the national federations with the exclusive jurisdiction and responsibility of forming independent arbitration tribunals at the national level. Article 63.5 of the FKF Statutes is a testament to this harmonious relationship, as it allows the FKF Appeals Committee to hear appeals against decisions passed by the IDAC.

260. In general, it is worth noting that the Kenyan sports associations are still evolving in as far as their dispute resolution bodies and procedures are concerned. Unlike the Kenyan civil courts, little is reported about the sports associations' tribunals first summoning the parties for hearings before issuing their decisions, although the parties have been afforded an opportunity to file written submissions.[17] It appears as though the decisions issued by the sports federation's internal bodies are usually rendered ex officio, with the members of the said tribunals only reported to have convened and deliberated.

V. Classification of Sports Disputes

261. From the Kenyan sports law perspective, a dispute of a purely sporting nature has been defined as that which involves the reviewing of contentious decisions rendered by referees or judges, or the application and interpretation of the playing laws of the game and has no economic connections or impact on the sports activity in question. Administrative and disciplinary disputes fall under this arm.

262. Disciplinary disputes would include appeals by players or clubs against sanctions, fines, suspensions or deduction of points meted out by sports federations in the course of a season for violating the laws of the game or the Federation's statutes.

263. On the other hand, one would naturally expect this definition of 'sporting nature' to mean that a contractual dispute between a Kenyan sports federation and a sponsoring company, or a dispute between a member of a sports body and a non-member ordinarily be filed before the Kenyan courts of law. Internal financial disputes involving the federation can also be referred to the national courts, because the element of 'specificity of sports' is not within them.

264. However, section 2 of the Kenyan Constitution provides that the constitution prevails over any other law in case of inconsistencies between the constitution and that other law.

---

17. In February 2013, Kenyan club Muhoroni Youth FC was fined Ksh 500,000 by the Kenyan Premier League for alleged incomplete registration of players contrary to the KPL Status and Transfer players policy. In its ruling, the KPL directed Muhoroni Youth FC to lodge its complaint to the IDAC for further directions on how to proceed with the appeal.

265. The conflicting provisions between the Constitution and the regulations of several sports bodies, such as those of the FKF have been the source of several disputes in relation to which body is competent to hear disputes wherein the parties are members of sports federations.

266. Whereas the FKF, with a view to avoiding sanctions from FIFA as its father body refrains from submitting disputes before the ordinary courts of law, other individual FKF members who have in one way or another been affected by the decision of the FKF have taken advantage of Article 2 of the Constitution and Article 48[18] of the Constitution, and filed proceedings before the ordinary courts of law in order to protect their individual rights. The Kenyan courts have not shied away in asserting their jurisdiction, as seen in the *Maina Kariuki v. FKF*.

VI. Decentralization of Disputes at Private Level

267. There is no central dispute resolution body charged with the responsibility of adjudicating all sports-related matters at private level.

268. It is implied that each sport has its own judicial internal dispute resolution bodies. Not all the sports, however, have such organs. Sports such as boxing, tennis, rugby and athletics do not have internal judicial bodies.

269. The situation is, however, different with the more popular sports like football and basketball which are becoming more and more professional. This has not only been caused as a result of the financial revenues and sponsorships but also a rise in the level of the player's knowledge in as far as their legal rights are concerned.

VII. The National Sports Disputes Tribunal

270. Pursuant to the Sports Act 2013, in May 2014, the Government revamped Kenya's dispute resolution system at private level by providing for the establishment of a centralized SDT in section 50.1 thereof.

A. *Composition of the National Sports Disputes Tribunal*

271. Pursuant to section 56.2 of the Sports Act 2013, the National Sports Disputes Tribunal consists of the following members appointed by Kenya's Judicial Service Commission in consultation with the national sports organizations:

---

18. Art. 48 of the Constitution accords every citizen the right to access justice by stating that 'The State shall ensure access to justice for all persons and, if any fee is required, it shall be reasonable and shall not impede access to justice.'

(a) a chairperson who shall be a person who is qualified to be appointed as a Judge of the High Court;
(b) at least two members who shall:
   – be advocates of the High Court of Kenya with at least seven years' experience;
   – have experience in legal matters relating to sports or have been involved in sport in any capacity; and
   – at least two and not more than six other persons who have experience in sport, in any capacity, of at least ten years.

272. In consultation with the national sports organizations, the Judicial Service Commission shall then appoint a deputy chairperson from the members of the National Sports Disputes Tribunal appointed under subsection (b) above.

273. The chairperson and members of the National Sports Disputes Tribunal hold office for a term of five years and may be reappointed for one further term of five years. Once appointed, they shall serve on a part-time basis.

274. Although Article 60 of the Sports Act states that '[t]he Tribunal may, in determining disputes apply alternative dispute resolution methods for sports disputes and provide expertise and assistance regarding alternative dispute resolution to the parties to a dispute', it is worth noting that the proposed Tribunal shares similar characteristics with that of an ordinary court rather than an independent arbitral body. Proving this is the fact that the judges are appointed by the Judicial Service Commission, with the associations or athletes having no say on which advocate they would prefer to sit on the bench. This is in sharp contrast with the arbitration, where the parties are free to choose arbitrators of their choice and may also challenge the appointment of any arbitrator or member of the panel. It is also not known whether the parties appearing before the National Sports Disputes Tribunal will enjoy the benefits of privacy and confidentiality of proceedings.

B. Jurisdiction of the National Sports Disputes Tribunal

275. Pursuant to section 59 of the Sports Act, the National Sports Disputes Tribunal is empowered to determine:

(a) appeals against decisions made by national sports organizations or umbrella national sports organizations, whose rules specifically allow for appeals to be made to the National Sports Disputes Tribunal in relation to that issue including:
   – appeals against disciplinary decisions;
   – appeals against not being selected for a Kenyan team or squad;
(b) other sports-related disputes that all parties to the dispute agree to refer to the National Sports Disputes Tribunal and that the national sports disputes tribunal agrees to hear; and
(c) appeals from decisions of the Registrar under the Sports Act.

Pursuant to Anti-Doping Bill 2016, the SDT can also entertain anti-doping matters as brought before it by ADAK.

C. Powers of the National Sports Disputes Tribunal

276. The National Sports Disputes Tribunal may, in determining disputes apply alternative dispute resolution methods for sports disputes and provide expertise and assistance regarding alternative dispute resolution to the parties to a dispute.

D. Rules Governing the National Sports Dispute Tribunal

277. The National Sports Tribunal is yet to have a code governing its rules and procedures. However, under section 62 of the Sports Act, the Chief Justice of Kenya may in consultation with the chairperson of the National Sports Disputes Tribunal, and by notice in the Gazette, make rules governing the practice and procedure of the National Sports Disputes Tribunal having regard to the objectives of the Sports Act.

E. Potential Government Interference Through the National Sports Disputes Tribunal

278. Whereas harmonious government support and assistance in the management and administration of sports is welcome and recognized under the Olympic Charter,[19] such support must not go beyond usurping the autonomy of the NOCK. Unfortunately, the Sports Act contains no provisions highlighting the relationship between the Parliament, the NOCK and the sports associations.

279. It is worth noting that the National Sports Disputes Tribunal is more of a government formed and operated tribunal rather than a tribunal established and run by the sports federations and led by the NOCK. In particular, the funds and assets of the proposed Tribunal shall 'comprise such moneys as may be appropriated by the Kenyan Parliament for purposes of Sports Kenya', which is a body established under the Sports Act.[20]

---

19. Art. 27.5 of the Olympic Charter 'In order to fulfil their mission, the NOCs may cooperate with governmental bodies, with which they shall achieve harmonious relations.'
20. Pursuant to Art. 4 of the Sports Act, Sports Kenya is a body corporate charged with the duty to: (a) establish and manage sports training academies; (b) organize, administer and coordinate sports courses for technical and sports administration personnel; (c) promote research and development of talent in sports, in collaboration with institutions of higher learning, national sports organizations and other stakeholders; (d) collect, collate, store and disseminate tangible and intangible historical sports material to the public, sports organizations, researchers and institutions of learning; (e) receive and analyse data on training requirements from sports organizations; (f) link with other institutions and organizations for regular updates on the current sports trends; and (g) perform any other function that may directly or indirectly contribute to the attainment of the foregoing.

280. Therefore, any members of the NOCK, and members of the NOCK who allow their internal decisions to be appealed to the proposed Tribunal risk being sanctioned by the IOC if it can be established that the decisions and operations of the proposed Tribunal interfere with the autonomy and independence of the NOCK and/or its members, in contravention with Article 27.6 of the Olympic Charter, which states that 'The NOCs must preserve their autonomy and resist all pressures of any kind, including but not limited to political, legal, religious or economic pressures which may prevent them from complying with the Olympic Charter.'

281. In addition, under Article 27.9 of the Olympic Charter:

> [t]he IOC Executive Board may take any appropriate decisions for the protection of the Olympic Movement in the country of an NOC, including suspension of or withdrawal of recognition from such NOC if the constitution, law or other regulations in force in the country concerned, or any act by any governmental or other body causes the activity of the NOC or the making or expression of its will to be hampered.

282. Therefore, the extent to which this substantially financed and wholly established governmental body shall act as Kenya's highest sports judicial body and administer sports justice without 'rubbing the shoulders' of the Olympic Committee remains to be seen, although its jurisdiction is mainly limited to hearing appeals against decisions made by national sports associations if the rules of the said associations specifically allow for appeals to be made to the proposed Tribunal.

283. It can also be argued that as a law in force in Kenya, section 59(a)(i) of the Sports Act risks causing the 'activity of the NOC or the making or expression of its will to be hampered' by allowing the National Sports Disputes Tribunal to entertain appeals filed by athletes who have been denied selection to be part of a Kenyan team or squad for the Olympics.

Chapter 1. History of Sports Betting in Kenya

284. Kenya is a country with a relatively short history, having attained its independence in 1963. Betting in sports was a relatively unknown activity prior to independence, and only began to develop in the early 1980s.

285. The practice has steadily picked up, and today there are numerous types of games involving betting in sports, such as horse racing, football, tennis and basketball.

286. Betting in Kenya is controlled by the Betting Control and Licensing Board, which was established by an Act of Parliament Chapter 131 Laws of Kenya in 1966. Prior to the Act, the functions of the board were handled by the Kenya Police Department. The Act provides for the control and licensing of betting and gaming premises and the activities carried thereon. It also provides for the authorization of lotteries and prize competitions as well as the eradication of illegal gambling.

287. Given the positive contributions, the gaming and betting industry continues to make for the economy in terms of employment and revenue generation, betting continues to become a legitimate consumer and hence the need for vigorous promotion and State supervision.

§1. The State Supervisory Mechanism

288. The Kenyan government plays a key role in the legal administration and controlling of betting activities in Kenyan sports. It does this through the establishment of various bodies, laws and stipulations of penalties, crimes and offences related to betting.

289. Among such laws and bodies are the Betting, Lotteries and Gaming Act, Chapter 131 Laws of Kenya and the Betting Control and Licensing Board.

290. Through these mechanisms, the Kenyan government has managed to protect and safeguard the public and third parties from unscrupulous betting operators while providing certain mandatory requirements related to licensing, ticketing, submission of returns, bookmaking and totalizing. Several betting institutions have also been established.

I. The Betting Lotteries and Gaming Act Chapter 131

291. This is the main legislation which caters for betting practices in Kenya. This Act comprises one of the many laws Kenya adopted from its colonizer, the UK. It has since undergone several amendments to suit the current practical conditions facing the Kenyan sports betting industry.

292. Section 2 of the Act defines betting as:

> to wager or stake any money or valuable thing by or on behalf of any person or, expressly or impliedly to undertake, promise or agree to wager or stake by or on behalf of any person, any money or valuable thing on a horse race, or other race, fight, game, sport, lottery or exercise or any other event or contingency.

293. The Act only recognizes betting activities which are carried out in public premises. It defines betting premises as 'premises to which the public has or may have access and which are kept or used (whether on one occasion or more than one) for the purpose of':

(a) bets being made therein between persons resorting to the premises and the owner, occupier or keeper thereof, or any person using the premises, or any person procured or employed by or acting for or on behalf of the owner, occupier, keeper or person using the premises, or of any person having the care or management or in any manner conducting the business thereof; or
(b) 'any money or valuable thing being received by or on behalf of the owner, occupier, keeper or person aforesaid as or for the consideration for any assurance, undertaking, promise or agreement, express or implied, to pay or give, or for securing the paying or giving by some other person of, any money or valuable thing on any horse race, or other race, fight, game, sport, lottery or exercise, or any other event or contingency'.

II. The Betting Control and Licensing Board

294. Whereas the Act principally sets out the formalities applicable to betting, and the duty to implement these formalities has been placed in the hands of a subordinate body.

295. The central body charged with the duty of foreseeing the administration and transparent operation of betting in Kenya is the Betting Control and Licensing Board. This board was established in 1966 and undertakes a number of functions.

A. Roles and Functions of the Betting Control and Licensing Board

296. The board's mission is to ensure that betting is conducted honestly and competitively with minimum costs but the maximum contribution to society, and that it is free from criminal activities.

297. It is charged with the responsibility of controlling and licensing of Betting and Gaming premises, facilitation of tax collection, authorization of public lotteries and prize competitions, inspection and elimination of illegal gambling.

B. Core Functions

298. The board performs a number of duties, among them, being:

(a) licensing and controlling of Betting and Gaming premises and the activities carried therein;
(b) authorization and control of prize competition and lotteries;
(c) curbing illegal betting, lotteries and gaming;
(d) providing an enabling environment for betting, lotteries and gaming;
(e) advocating for betting, lotteries and gaming as a legitimate consumer pursuit; and
(f) creating awareness and public confidence in betting, lotteries and gaming.

III. Requirements and Conditions for Operating Betting Premises

299. The Betting, Lotteries and Gaming Act empowers the National Betting Control and Licensing Board to impose such conditions as it may deem necessary to ensure that lotteries are promoted and conducted as efficiently as possible, in the interest of the purpose for which it was being promoted, of the public in general.

300. Pursuant to this, the Board has come up with a number of requirements to which all lottery operators must adhere. In order to operate and carry out the business of sports betting in Kenya, an individual or company must meet the following conditions:

(a) he or she must acquire a betting licence;
(b) operators must have tickets; and
(c) they must submit their returns.

A. Licensing Requirement

301. A person who wishes to run the business of sports betting in Kenya must apply for a licence. The application must be submitted to the board in duplicate and be accompanied with a minimal application fee. The licences are valid for one year and must be renewed by the end of the thirtieth day of June of the following year.

302. In accordance with section 5(3)(1) of the Betting Lotteries and Gaming Act, an applicant may be denied a licence if a number of conditions have not been met, such as:

(a) If he or she fails to satisfy the Board that he or she is a fit and proper person to hold the licence or permit and that the premises, if any, in respect of which the application is made are suitable for the purpose.

(b) If the applicant knowingly makes a false statement or declaration in an application for, or a renewal or variation of, a licence or permit.[21]
(c) If the Board fails to send a copy of the application for the licence to the local authority within whose area of the jurisdiction where the applicant proposes to conduct his business and has given the local authority reasonable opportunity to object to, or make recommendations with respect to, the application.

B. Duties of a Sports Betting Licence Holder

303. Upon receiving a betting licence, the holder thereof is required to perform and abide by a number of duties.

304. To begin with, in case a licensee changes the name, address or location of a business to which the licence relates, or in case he performs any change that affects his interest as an owner, director, partner, agent, manager or servant in that business, he must, within seven days of the aforesaid change.

305. Licensees who close down their business must give written notice to the Board within seven days of closure and must surrender their licence to the Board.[22]

306. Failure to observe any of these regulations exposes the licensee to a fine not exceeding Ksh 100 or to imprisonment for a term not exceeding one month or both.

C. Ticketing Requirement

307. The Betting Lotteries and Gaming Act requires those who run betting premises to operate with tickets.

308. In accordance with section 5.1 of the Betting Lotteries and Gaming Act, the Board is required to cause books of tickets to be printed and numbered serially for sale to bookmakers at a cost equal to the costs of production.

309. The Betting Lotteries and Gaming Act requires any bookmaker who takes a bet at a place other than at an authorized race meeting to issue the person from whom he has taken the bet a ticket from one of the books of tickets. He or she must thereafter enter the particulars of the bet on the ticket.

310. Section 5.4 of the Betting Lotteries and Gaming Act makes it an offence for a bookmaker to place a bet at a place other than an authorized racing meeting and to thereafter fail to issue a ticket.

---

21. Such an act invites a fine not exceeding Ksh 50,000 or to imprisonment for a term not exceeding six months or to both.
22. *See* s. 16(3) cap 131 of the Betting, Lotteries and Gaming Regulations.

D. *Submission of Returns*

311. All lottery operators are required to submit returns on a quarterly basis, showing details of the number of tickets printed, the number of tickets sold, the cost of each ticket to the public, the amount of money collected, the amount of money devoted to a good cause, the amount of money one ascribes, the names of all the winners, the names of all the beneficiaries and the amount received by each presiding and supervision of all lottery draws by the board of officials.

312. Records must also be kept of all draw results published in the media and provision be made guaranteeing to cover the prices to be awarded in the lottery; the board officials must also witness the awarding of prizes won in the lottery.

IV. Illegal and Prohibited Betting Activities

313. Like with any other activity, betting in Kenya can lead to a number of offences. The following betting activities have been declared illegal and are subject to sanctions in Kenya:

(a) Betting with young persons.
(b) Betting in public.
(c) Betting at unauthorized places.
(d) Operating without a licence.
(e) Betting in unlicensed premises.
(f) Public invitation to unlicensed premises.
(g) Reception and/or advancement of money at unlicensed premises.

A. *Betting with Young Persons*

314. Under section 28.1 of the Betting Lotteries and Gaming Act, a person who:

(a) bets with a young person; or
(b) employs a young person on licensed betting premises or in connection with a pool betting scheme; or
(c) receives or negotiates a bet through a young person; or
(d) sends to a young person any circular, notice, advertisement, letter or other document relating to betting.

Shall be guilty of an offence and liable to a fine not exceeding Ksh 30,000 or to imprisonment for a term not exceeding three months, or to both.

'Young person' has been defined as a person who is under the age of 18.

B. Betting in Public

315. It is an offence for any person to frequent or loiter in a street or public place, on behalf either of himself or of any other person, for the purposes of bookmaking, betting, agreeing to bet, or paying, receiving or settling bets. This offence invites a fine not exceeding Ksh 50,000 or imprisonment for a term not exceeding six months or both.

C. Betting at Unauthorized Places

316. As seen earlier, under section 5.4 of the Betting, Gaming and Lotteries Regulations, it is an offence for a bookmaker to place a bet at a place other than an authorized racing meeting and then fail to issue a ticket. This offence carries a penalty of a fine not exceeding Ksh 5,000 or to a term of imprisonment for a term not exceeding six months, or to both.[23]

D. Operating without a Licence

317. Section 14.1(a) of the Betting Lotteries and Gaming Act makes it clear that an owner or occupier of a betting premises, or any person having temporary use or otherwise thereof, who keeps or uses unlicensed betting premises is guilty of an offence and liable to a fine not exceeding Ksh 10,000 or to imprisonment for a term not exceeding one year or to both.

318. Case laws in Kenya are few and far between. However, in the *criminal Case No. 1962 of 2006 Jackson Kioko, Muia Mutinda, Joseph Muthama and Mwanzia Kioko v. The Republic*,[24] the four accused were charged with gambling in a public place without a valid licence. They were sentenced, on their own plea of guilty, to each pay a fine of Ksh 5,000 in default of which they would all serve two months imprisonment.

E. Betting in Unlicensed Premises

319. A person who bets in unlicensed betting premises shall be guilty of an offence and liable to a fine not exceeding Ksh 5,000 or to a term of imprisonment for a term not exceeding six months, or to both. On a similar note, a person found in unlicensed betting premises or found escaping there from on the occasion of their being entered shall be presumed, until the contrary is proved, to be or to have been betting therein.

23. *See* s. 14.2 of the Betting Lotteries and Gaming Act.
24. *See* http://www.kenyalaw.org/CaseSearch/case_search_fts.php?words=BETTING+%26+LICENCING+&check_submit=1&submitter=SEARCH+%BB&mode=normal.

320. People under whose care or management an unlicensed betting premise has been left can also be guilty of an offence if they in any manner assist or are knowingly engaged in the management of such unlicensed premises. They may be liable to a fine not exceeding Ksh 5,000 or to imprisonment for a term not exceeding six months or both.

F. Public Invitation to Unlicensed Premises

321. Innocent third parties should also be on the lookout as the Act makes it an offence for any person to announce, publish or cause to be announced or published, either orally or by means of any print, writing, design, sign or otherwise, that premises are opened, kept or used as unlicensed betting premises, or in any manner to invite or solicit any person to bet in unlicensed betting premises.

322. Any such act renders the person liable to a fine not exceeding Ksh 10,000 or to imprisonment for a term not exceeding one year or to both.

G. Reception and/or Advancement of Money at Unlicensed Premises

323. Under section 14(e) of the Betting Lotteries and Gaming Act, the advancement, furnishment or reception of money by any person for the purpose of establishing or conducting the business of unlicensed betting premises is prohibited. Any such act renders the person liable to a fine not exceeding Ksh 10,000 or to imprisonment for a term not exceeding one year or to both.

H. Other Offences

324. Touting, that is, the displaying of advertisements, printouts, notices or public placards by persons holding themselves out as being ready and willing to bet with members of the public is also prohibited and invites jail terms of up to three months.[25]

325. Section 43 of the Betting Lotteries and Gaming Act also criminalizes the selling or promotion of lottery tickets to minors below the age of 16 years, with those found guilty of doing so likely to face either fines or sentences not exceeding Ksh 3,000, or three months respectively, or both. However, any promoter or sports organizer who sells such tickets may plead in defence, that the offence occurred without his consent or connivance and that he exercised all due diligence to prevent it, or that he neither knew nor had reasonable cause to suspect that the person he sold the tickets to was under the age of 16.

25. Section 25 of the Betting Lotteries and Gaming Act.

I. Protection of Third Parties and the Public

326. The Betting Lotteries and Gaming Act goes further to protect private, public entities as well as members of the public from exploitation by unscrupulous licence holders and gives them greater security in their dealings with betting businesses. It does this through several regulations, which it has put in place:

J. Furnishing Monetary Security

327. All applicants are required to furnish the Board with security by means of a deposit, or such other security as the Board may approve, of a sum not exceeding Ksh 40,000. This security is meant to cater for any immediate financial damages which a licence holder could cause to third parties. It is thereafter refunded or cancelled on the expiration or cancellation of the licence.[26]

328. In determining the amount of security, the Board takes into account:

(1) the known business of the applicant;
(2) the amount, if any, by which that business may reasonably be expected to increase in the ensuing year; and
(3) the Board may at any time vary the amount of any security given in pursuance of this section if it is satisfied that, having regard to the known scale of business of the licensee concerned, the variation is reasonable. (sections 6(3) and (4) of the Betting Lotteries and Gaming Act).

329. It is intended that through this, the public can have greater confidence while dealing with betting operators.

K. Prominent Displaying of Licences

330. All licence holders are required to prominently display their licences on conspicuous areas of their principal place of business and on any part thereof to which the public has access. In addition, a copy of such licence must be similarly displayed at each of the branches of the licensee or permit-holder.[27]

331. Failure to do this, or displaying of an invalid licence by the licence holder in question renders him liable to pay a fine not exceeding Ksh 3,000, or to imprisonment for a term not exceeding three months or to both.

26. *See* s. 6 of the Betting Lotteries and Gaming Act.
27. *See* s. 8 of the Betting Lotteries and Gaming Act.

L. Prohibition of Retransfer of Licences

332. Section 12 of the Betting Lotteries and Gaming Act prohibits the transfer to another person, of any licence issued to him. A person who transfers or purports to transfer a licence or permit is guilty of an offence and liable to a fine not exceeding Ksh 2,000 or to imprisonment for a term not exceeding two months, or to both.

§2. BOOKMAKING AND TOTALIZING

333. The Betting Lotteries and Gaming Act does have a place for bookmakers engaged in the business of betting. It defines a bookmaker as:

> a person who, whether on his own account or as servant or agent to another person, carries on, whether occasionally or regularly, the business of receiving or negotiating bets, or who in any manner holds himself out, or permits himself to be held out in any manner, as a person who receives or negotiates bets.[28]

334. Bookmakers and totalizers in Kenya may be issued with two types of licences; an on-the-course licence[29] or an off-the-course licence[30] or both. The totalizers' licences may be limited to either each race day or for a period not exceeding one year.

335. The licences shall act as authority, enabling them to carry on the business as bookmakers but only at the betting premises named thereon. In addition, bookmakers may also carry out their business in the form of partnerships and must keep a full and accurate record of all betting transactions entered into.

336. Bookmaking without a valid licence invites a fine not exceeding Ksh 10,000 or imprisonment for a term not exceeding one year, or to both.

I. Documents and Records to Be Kept by Bookmakers

337. Bookmakers and totalizers are required to file their returns within seven days following each period of fourteen days.

338. In addition to this, all bookmakers in the Kenyan sports industry are required to keep a full and accurate record of all betting transactions entered into showing:

---

28. http://kenyalaw.org/kl/.
29. This licence authorizes a person to carry on his business as a bookmaker at any authorized race meeting.
30. This licence authorizes a person to carry on his business as a bookmaker at the betting premises named therein.

(a) the total amount of bets received by him (including bets received at an authorized race meeting), and the total amount of winnings paid by him; and
(b) in the case of bets received at a place other than an authorized race meeting, the total amount of losing bets and the total amount of winning bets.

339. In addition to (a) and (b) above, totalizers must keep records showing the amount of money devoted to any charitable purposes or other purposes and must, within twenty-one days after each race on which that totalizer was operated, submit to the Permanent Secretary a certified statement in duplicate together with a remittance for the amount of the tax due.[31]

II. Conclusion

340. The Kenyan government does have control over the activities of betting in sports events. Evidence of this is seen through the Act and in the criminal sanctions imposable on persons who engage in betting activities without licences.

341. All said and done, greater efforts need to be put in place to further streamline the laws. Public awareness and education on betting in sports must also be carried out, with emphasis on the possible illegalities involved in betting, the consequences thereof, and on promoting safe and healthy betting practices.

342. Sports possess great potential for fostering development. The public and the private community must therefore be encouraged to participate in sports activities, of which betting is one, with a view to promoting the economy.

343. With the increasing popularity, internet access and creation of new games in betting, it is only a matter of time before Kenya, with the help of more tranquillized legislations, maximizes its income as a State from betting collections.

31. *See* s. 8 of the Betting, Lotteries and Gaming Regulations.

Chapter 2. Trademarks, Corporate and Merchandizing

344. Branding and merchandising is fast-growing within the Kenyan sports market. Of all the sports, football is way ahead, having gathered corporate, intellectual property and commercial pace with impressive success.

345. The law governing intellectual property, and to some extent, corporate and merchandising related issues in Kenya is the Trade Marks Act cap 506. There is no specific law which governs issues related to merchandising per se, whose activities are intertwined in between the Law of Contract Act, the Companies Act, the Trade Marks Act and the Competition Act, among other, laws.

346. The Trade Marks Act has undergone several amendments to conform to worldwide trends with the most recent amendments such as Legal Notice No. 145 of Kenya brought into force the Madrid Protocol by the enactment of the Trade Marks (International Registration) Rules, 2003.

347. The Trade Marks Act also incorporates provisions relating to the protection of well-known marks as recommended by the World Intellectual Property Organization (WIPO). Kenya is also a party to the Nice Agreement concerning the International Classification of Goods and Services for the purposes of the registration of trademarks.

348. The Trade Marks Act defines a 'mark' as including 'a distinguishing guise, slogan, device, brand, heading, label, ticket, name, signature, word, letter or numeral or any combination thereof whether rendered in two-dimensional or three-dimensional form'.

349. Under section 6(1) of the Trade Marks Act, '[a] trade mark shall be registered in respect of particular goods or services (…)'.

§1. Duration and Renewal of Trademark Registration

350. The trademark is valid for a period of ten years. This is expressly stipulated under section 23.1 of the Trade Marks Act, which states that '[t]he registration of a trade mark shall be for a period of ten years, but may be renewed from time to time in accordance with the provisions of this section'.

The Extent of Rights

351. In accordance with section 7.1 of the Trade Marks Act, '[a] trade mark if valid gives to that person the exclusive right to the use of the trade mark in relation to the goods or in connection with the provision of any services'.

352. Without prejudice to the generality of the foregoing, a trademark right is infringed by any person who, not being the proprietor of the trademark or a registered user thereof using by way of permitted use, uses a mark identical with or so nearly resembling it as to be likely to deceive or cause confusion in the course of trade or in connection with the provision of any services in respect of which it is registered, and in such manner as to render the use of the mark likely to:

(a) be taken either as being used as a trademark;
(b) be taken in a case in which the use is upon the goods or in physical relation thereto or in an advertising circular or other advertisement issued to the public, as importing a reference to some person having the right either as proprietor or as a licensee to use the trademark or goods with which such a person is connected in the course of trade;
(c) be taken in a case where the user is used at or near the place where the services are available for acceptance or performed or in an advertising circular or other advertisement issued to the public or any part thereof, as importing a reference to some person having the right either as proprietor or as a licensee to use the trademark or to services with the provision of which such a person as aforesaid is connected in the course of business;
(d) cause injury or prejudice to the proprietor or licensee of the trademark.

§2. Image Rights

353. It is fast becoming a reality in the world of sport that athletes earn substantial income not only from their on-field performances, but also from the valuable sponsorship deals and endorsements concluded between them and the vendors of certain goods or services.

354. However, image right contracts have not quite hit the scene in Kenyan sports due to a number of factors. The main reason is of course the fact that apart from athletes engaged in long and middle distance running, most local sportsmen are not regarded that 'famous' in Kenya, as they are still in their amateur and/or development stages. They hence attract little or no interest from the public and private entities which might want to secure their image rights.

355. Moreover, an inquest into the professional contracts of most sportsmen, especially those engaged in football, reveals no clause under which they agree to vest their image rights in favour of their clubs. It is therefore implied that although these players are still unknown or, they hold 100% of their image rights despite having signed employment contracts with their clubs.

356. Having said the above, it is worth noting that Kenyan law does not currently recognize any specific proprietary interest and property rights in the image, likeness, voice or other aspects of the persona of individuals such as famous sports stars or celebrities.

357. Where sports stars themselves or through their image companies have registered their image rights as trademarks, infringement proceedings may be instituted against the infringer for such trademark infringement.

Chapter 3. Broadcasting of Sports Events

§1. Freedom of Media

358. Under Article 34.1 of the Kenyan Constitution, all media and broadcasters, journalists and press are guaranteed the freedom and independence of electronic, print and all other types of media.

§2. Public Interest and Right to Information

359. The Kenya Information and Communications Act requires all broadcasters to commit a minimum amount of time as in their programme schedule to locally produced programmes, or, in the alternative, pay such amount of money as may be prescribed into a fund to assist the development of the Kenyan production industry.

360. Section 14.1 of the Kenya Broadcasting Corporation Chapter 221 Laws of Kenya vests the Kenya Broadcasting Corporation as the sole TV station with the right to broadcast programmes of national importance. In this regard, the Kenya Broadcasting Corporation has continued to air all sporting within or outside Kenya events involving the Kenyan national team.

The Major Events of Public Interest:

- The FKF cup finals.
- The African cup of nations.
- The Olympics.
- The World Cup.
- The World Athletics Championships.
- The African Athletics Championships.

§3. Licensing

361. Section 35.1 of the Kenya Information and Communications Act Chapter 411 Laws of Kenya requires all radio stations to have licences issued by the Communications Commission of Kenya in order to carry out their activities. Section 46C(1) contains a similar provision in relation to broadcasting stations.

362. It is worth noting that local leagues and competitions such as the Kenyan premier league have their own private TV sponsorship deals and as such the Kenya Broadcasting Corporation does not broadcast local leagues for free.

Chapter 4. Sports and COVID in Kenya

§1. Suspension of Sporting Activities

363. The Kenyan government suspended all sporting activities in April 2020 following the outbreak of the COVID-19 pandemic in Kenya.

364. In football, FKF cancelled the Kenyan Premier League (the top tier league) and the National Super League (the second-tier league) on 30 April 2020 and scrapped the rest of the five tiers of football.

In August 2020, the Government issued draft guidelines for the resumption of sporting activities which include, among others:

(a) A COVID-19 test on athletes seventy-two hours before competition.
(b) At the match venue: health checks, body temperature checks and screening for players, officials, venue staff, sports goods suppliers and any other persons entering the venue.;
(c) The appointment by the FKF and/or the league organizers and venue operators of COVID-19 contact persons and response teams.
(d) Availability of handwashing facilities, sanitizers and thermometers at the training and competition sites.
(e) No sharing of water bottles and other drinking devices, hugs and no handshakes, exchange or sharing of uniforms during matches.
(f) Replacing press conferences for players with flash interviews conducted respecting the social distancing of 1.5 meters and more.
(g) The wearing of face masks by all but active athletes and event officials during matches.
(h) Players to resume training in three phases:
    (i) Phase 1: dedicated to medical and athletic tests (three to four days).
    (ii) Phase 2: players to resume training individually for seven days before training in small groups for a week.
    (iii) Phase 3: team training.

§2. Stimulus Measures

365. In April 2020, the Government introduced a number of stimulus measures aimed at cushioning the country as a whole such as:

(i) Tax relief for employees who earn a gross salary of less than Ksh 24,000 per month to give them extra cash to help cope with the crisis.
(ii) Reducing income tax from 30 to 25%, and corporate tax from 30 to 25%

366. In addition, the Ministry of Sports asked FKF to furnish them with a list of 30 members (25 players and 5 officials) of the clubs participating in the national leagues (including the Women Premier League) with a view to paying them an undisclosed amount of money to cushion them during the pandemic.

367. On 26 May 2020, the Government rolled out a Ksh 20 million COVID-19 stimulus package from which it announced that every KPL player will be paid Ksh 10,000 for the next three months to help ease their burdens during the pandemic.

§3. Broadcast Sponsorship

368. In August 2021, FKF lost its league broadcaster, StarTimes, after they terminated their contract with the federation. The grounds were not based on the pandemic, although StarTimes cited frustration and several contractual breaches of the sponsorship deal by FKF.

§4. Pay Cuts/Suspension of Salaries for Football Players

369. Prior to the pandemic, a significant number of players especially those contracted to the self-sponsored/community-based clubs already had their salaries in substantial arrears (some dating as far back as five months). It is little wonder that some of those clubs did not bother asking their players to take pay cuts or deferrals given that prior to the pandemic, the players in question already had salary arrears running into four to five months. A number of struggling clubs resorted to paying their players handouts or pocket money to cushion them through the pandemic.

370. The more stable clubs like Kakamega Homeboyz FC announced that their players had agreed to a 50% pay cut. Another club, Western Stima FC also followed suit and announced that its players would take a 50% pay cut, although the players later denied any agreement and claimed that the cuts had been imposed.

371. Corporate funded clubs such as Tusker FC, Bandari FC and Kenya Commercial Bank FC continued paying their players in full.

> Section 17 of the Employment Act No. 11 of 2007 laws of Kenya provides for the protection of wages by stating that an employer shall pay the entire amount of the wages earned by or payable to an employee in respect of work done by the employee in pursuance of a contract of service directly … .[32]

372. Pay cuts owing to *force majeure* events such as COVID-19 could only be done with the employee's consent.

373. Whether or not a contract can be terminated for *force majeure* depends on its wording. Some contracts provide for termination, while others provide for the suspension of obligations.

32. http://kenyalaw.org/kl/.

The mere fact that an employer is unable to perform the contract or because doing so has become more expensive does not necessarily amount to a *force majeure*. The employer must show that he/she has explored all other avenues of performing the contract without success.

§5. Partial Return to 'Normalcy'

374. In November 2020, the Kenyan government allowed all low-risk contact sports, and national teams to resume their activities. All other activities related to lower-level leagues remain suspended.

375. No spectators were allowed at any sporting event, and all federations were required to ensure compliance with all the provisions of the guidelines.

Full Resumption to 'Normalcy'

376. In October 2021, the Government paved the way for a return to 'normalcy' by lifting the ban on closed-door sporting activities, thereby allowing stadiums and venues in the country to operate at full capacity.

Selected Bibliography

Codes.
Sports Act 2013.
Kenyalaw.org.
Articles.
The Evolution of Bad Governance in Kenyan Sports by Adili, a fortnightly news service produced by TI-Kenya's Communications Programme.
Sports Newspapers.
Nation Media Group Kenya Limited.
East African Standard Group Kenya Limited.

Index

The numbers here refer to paragraph numbers.

Index

www.ingramcontent.com/pod-product-compliance
Ingram Content Group UK Ltd.
Pitfield, Milton Keynes, MK11 3LW, UK
UKHW020150290926
15471UKWH00004B/786

9 789403 500461